BEING
LIVING KOREA

BEING KOREAN, LIVING KOREA

THROUGH MY LENS

Donyeob Kim

Copyright © 2024 Donyeob Kim

All rights reserved.

ISBN: 9798301331107

To my beloved Kate and Seo-jun,
I dedicate this book.

CONTENTS

1. On The Street 1
2. What We Eat 43
3. I Am From 57
4. Four Kingdoms over Twenty Centuries 69
5. True Freedom Beyond Anti-communism 80
6. Rich out of Poverty 87
7. Believer Below 40% 95
8. One-Size-Fits-None Education 105
9. Beyond The Uniform 111
10. Go-To Getaway 119
About The Author 126
Notes 127

Foreword

Sometimes, while traveling, I wonder about the lives of people there. What kind of work do the Americans in Buffalo Grove, an hour's drive from Chicago, do out there, away from the bustle of the city? Why was that woman jogging alone in the middle of the day on Route 604 near Norway's remote Nigardsbreen Glacier? I wonder how stressful it must be to find parking for people in Manarola, one of Italy's Cinque Terre towns. Or, for the people of Paris—do they also have to ask their children to wait when they suddenly need a bathroom break on the street?

I want to hear the stories of ordinary people—not the tales from busy tourist spots, but the lives of those living day after day in quieter cities. YouTube is too loud and too busy, like a tourist attraction. Standing there feels like facing a whole herd of zebras as a lone lion—confusing. Even when the algorithm tries to act as a tour guide, it is easy to feel lost.

This book is my way of sharing the ordinary stories I have wanted to hear.

What kind of country is Korea, the place I live? Here in Korea, there are a few dozen people I keep in regular contact with, a few hundred more I have met before, and tens of millions I will likely never meet. My world may be small, but I grew up in Korea and have experienced everyday life here. I have been both a country mouse and a city mouse. I went to school in a rural area and studied hard to move beyond it. Luckily, I made it to Seoul and attended a well-known university. During my studies, I completed my mandatory military service (as is typical for Korean men, who typically serve while in college). After graduating, I started my career without much delay. In my early 30s, I married and had a child. Like many other parents, I greatly focus on my child's education.

This book is a glimpse into life in Korea, told from an ordinary perspective. I will begin lightly by walking you through the city and sharing what I notice. After this tour, I will discuss Korean food as hunger sets in. Once we have filled up, I will move on to the less visible aspects of Korean life—Korea and Korean, history, democracy and politics, economy, religion, education, and military & North Korea—and finally wrap up with travel.

Through these stories, you will understand Korea better.

1

On The Street

Road

"*Right Now, Wrong Then*" is the title of a famous 2015 film by director Hong Sang-soo. This phrase perfectly captures the idea of shifting perspectives and works just as well in reverse ("Wrong Now, Right Then"). The most common street tree in Seoul is the ginkgo. In autumn, roads lined with ginkgo trees turn bright yellow, and the sky looks extra blue through their golden leaves. With their distinctive fan-shaped leaves, children often collect ginkgo leaves and press them into books alongside four-leaf clovers. But there is a unique challenge with these trees, which have male and female versions like animals do: the problem is their troublesome "offspring"—their fruits. When ginkgo fruits fall on the sidewalks, they emit a strong odor, and pedestrians quickly find themselves dodging these "bombs" scattered under the trees. Have you ever seen a street tree with a net shaped like an upside-down triangle under its branches? The net is to catch the ginkgo fruits before they fall to the ground. Responding to complaints from citizens, the Seoul city government fights an annual "war" against the ginkgo trees, installing nets or using machines to shake the fruits down. Still, it seems no one can genuinely defeat the ginkgo in autumn.

So, why were ginkgo trees chosen as street trees despite these issues? The answer is simple: "Wrong Now, Right Then." Ginkgo trees were a popular choice because of their resilience—they are not only resistant to pests but also cope well with pollution, making them ideal for city streets. However, back then, technology had not advanced enough to distinguish male and female ginkgo from young seedlings, which is why we have both types today.

Something is always happening on the roads, but it moves so slowly that it is hard to notice. At some point, old cars started disappearing from the streets, replaced only by new ones. With rising incomes, people are more inclined to buy and replace newer cars more frequently. So, where have all the old cars gone? They are often sent to the countryside, packed into dark containers, and shipped abroad. If you look closer at the cars passing by, you will also notice that bright, flashy colors are rare. Many Koreans avoid buying cars in vivid colors because they do not want to stand out, and such cars have low resale value, making them hard to sell at a reasonable price later. Today, almost all the new cars on the road are Korean-made. German brands like Mercedes and BMW used to draw attention in the past, but now Korean models are turning heads. Domestic cars are more stylish and have improved their performance, and they sell well internationally, too. (Hyundai Motor Group, which includes Hyundai Motor and Kia, was ranked among the top three global car sellers as of 2022.)

We might soon start seeing bold, flashy advertisements right on the sidewalks at crosswalks. Nowadays, Koreans of all ages tend to pull out their smartphones when they stop, and waiting at a crosswalk is no exception. Absorbed in their screens, they often miss the green light unless they look up. For the safety of these "tech neck" pedestrians, more crosswalks are now equipped with long LED signals embedded in the ground, helping them see the lights without looking up.

City

Korean cities change rapidly, driven by competing ambitions and survival pressures. You will likely lose yourself if you return to Korea after five years and try to navigate based on old memories. Even as a resident, I need help to keep up with the ever-changing urban landscape. So, why do cities in Korea transform so often? Here is why.

First, the city's appearance is shaped by local government officials, particularly mayors, whose political careers depend on visible achievements. In Korea, reelection is crucial, so politicians need accomplishments that catch voters' eyes. They have seen how former Seoul Mayor Lee Myung-bak's restoration of the Cheonggyecheon Stream helped him rise to the presidency. As a result, they often prioritize high-visibility urban renewal over less noticeable welfare projects.

Second, replacing older buildings requires substantial funding. Where does this money come from? Since the global financial crisis, Korea has maintained low interest rates, making returns on traditional investments less appealing. Institutional investors—such as pension funds and insurance companies—have sought higher yields, leading them to pour capital into real estate funds that have fueled Korea's property boom. This influx of capital has transformed many older buildings, especially in central business districts, into new developments.

Finally, small business owners are in an ongoing struggle to survive in this shifting environment. Competition is fierce—1.6 restaurants for every 100 people indicates saturation. When one restaurant does well, similar low-cost franchises open nearby, quickly siphoning off customers. Additionally, rent is a challenge for small businesses; in Korea, rental payments are typically fixed and not tied to revenue, making it challenging to manage rising costs if sales stay flat. Other burdens, like high interest rates, labor costs, and delivery platform fees, add to the strain. According to a report by the Korea Consumer Agency, the five-year survival rate for businesses in the lodging and restaurant sector is just 22.8%. In many ways, small business owners' struggles continuously reshape the face of the city.

Trash bin

Trash bins are difficult to find in Seoul. As a salaried worker, I pay taxes not only to the national government but also to the local government, which takes an additional 10% of my income tax as local tax. Even though I dutifully contribute to national and local coffers, sometimes I resent the local government and feel my tax money is wasted when I realize there is no place to throw away the trash in my hand while walking down the street. These days, finding a trash bin on the streets is as tricky as finding a needle in a haystack.

This inconvenience, however, is not an old tradition. Finding a trash bin on the streets was easy when I did not pay taxes. However, when Korea introduced a pay-as-you-throw waste system, trash bins disappeared individually. So, what does this waste system do with the vanishing street trash bins? To avoid paying for household waste disposal, some people began dumping their home trash into street bins, leading local governments to remove public bins altogether. While Seoul has recently started addressing citizens' complaints by reintroducing trash bins in certain areas, it is still insufficient.

Despite the lack of bins, the streets remain

remarkably clean. Part of this is due to heightened public awareness, discouraging people from littering. But it is also because people other than sanitation workers are picking up litter. In Korea, it is common for parents to financially support their children well into adulthood, including through marriage, often leaving themselves unprepared for retirement. As a result, many elderly citizens experience financial insecurity. To help, local governments employ elderly individuals part-time, offering them modest pay to collect litter from the streets. Behind Seoul's clean streets lies a hidden story of elderly poverty.

Habits are compelling. In Korea, the pay-as-you-throw waste system has been in place since 1995, and food waste separation has been mandatory since 2013. After more than a decade of separating food waste from general trash, putting both into the same garbage bag feels completely strange. This would never happen in Korea, no matter where you go. However, when staying at an Airbnb abroad, I occasionally face the uncomfortable situation of putting them together in one bag. As a result, I set food waste aside in a separate bag.

Coffee shop

Koreans have coffee after every meal, treating caffeine almost as a digestive aid. Suppose you walk through the busy streets of Seoul's Yeouido business district during lunch hour. In that case, you will notice nearly everyone carrying a disposable cup of coffee.

Koreans love iced coffee. There is even a coined term in Korean: "Eol-juk-ah," which translates to "Iced Americano till I freeze to death." This term sums up Koreans' dedication to iced coffee, regardless of the temperature outside. But why do Koreans choose iced coffee, forgoing the aroma of a hot coffee? Part of the answer lies in Korean food, which often includes spicy, hot dishes. To balance the intense flavors, Koreans tend to prefer refreshing cold drinks, including water, alcohol, and, of course, coffee. For instance, the waitstaff often serves chilled bottled water from the refrigerator. While somebody may ask for hot water or coffee, lukewarm beer or soju is almost unheard of here—Koreans even enjoy whiskey on the rocks.

Koreans' fondness for coffee is not new, but the type of coffee in fashion has changed. The first coffee trend in Korea featured instant coffee, often stored in glass jars. When guests visited, it was customary for the host to heat water and serve coffee, often with unique cups reflecting the family's style and budget. Coffee cup sets were a popular gift back then. Hosts would mix coffee, sugar, and a powdery creamer in the cup, sometimes adjusting the amounts according to the guests' preferences. The specific ratios used at each household made every home-brewed coffee taste slightly different. Later, instant coffee made at home was replaced by a premade recipe: single-serving coffee mix sticks became widely available, letting people enjoy coffee simply by adding hot water to paper cups. Around this time, coffee vending machines also popped up in urban areas, offering an affordable and tasty brew for just 100 Korean Won (about 10 cents), a price that is hard to imagine now. Brewed coffee from coffee makers held sway for a while in coffee shops, and older styles of instant coffee shops known as "dabang" gradually faded. The coffee Koreans enjoy today, brewed from espresso machines, became mainstream when Starbucks arrived in Korea. The large mugs of black coffee and American pop culture left a strong impression on Koreans. Traditionally, coffee in Korea was cheap and sweet, while American-style coffee was more bitter, rich, and notably fragrant. Young Koreans, a generation with strong purchasing power and a taste for unique experiences, embraced American-style coffee culture, transforming coffee into a cultural staple in Korea.

Although Starbucks is one of Korea's favorite coffee shops, it does not dominate the market as it does in the U.S. Numerous large Korean beverage and retail companies have launched their successful coffee chains inspired by Starbucks' model. Starbucks was among the pricier coffee options at one point, but now its prices seem moderate compared to other major coffee chains that have increased their prices significantly. Recently, due to the impact of high inflation, low-cost coffee chains like Mega Coffee have become increasingly popular.

These days, coffee shops are increasing the number of single-person seats. Many people find it easier to focus when reading a book in a coffee shop or on the subway, where there's just the right amount of white noise. Because of this, more people are choosing to study at coffee shops, and they've even earned the nickname "Ka-gong-jok" or "café study tribe." However, conflicts sometimes arise when some of these café study tribes complain that other customers are too noisy. It feels a bit unfair that people must be mindful of others, even though coffee shops are originally meant to be places for conversation.

Study café

Cafés in Korea are usually on the first floor, but if you see a Café sign on the second or third floor, it is likely a study café. When a regular café is too noisy to focus, a study café is the perfect alternative. Despite the name, study cafés are not typical social coffee spots—they are quiet spaces where people, especially students, go to concentrate on their work. A small kitchenette provides a variety of complimentary beverages, including coffee, which is how these spaces earn their "café" title. Conversation and phone calls are prohibited inside, and each seat is partitioned to block distractions. In short, it's an ideal environment for focused work.

While students make up the majority of study café customers, adults preparing for exams or business projects are also frequent visitors. Study cafés are open 24 hours a day and generally operate without staff.

Payment is usually made via kiosk. Free Wi-Fi is, of course, provided. Home, with all its comforts, often invites procrastination. In contrast, this controlled space offers the ideal setting to tackle long-postponed tasks like writing this book for me.

Bakery

Just as Westerners have long revered wheat, Koreans have historically held rice in high esteem. However, as noodles and bread gain popularity, this reverence for rice is slowly becoming a relic of the past. Declining rice and rising wheat consumption is now so commonplace that it barely makes the news. Michael Pollan writes in *The Omnivore's Dilemma*, "They say you are what you eat. If that's true, then most of us are essentially corn." Pollan refers to how scientists can determine the diets of ancient humans through their remains and suggests the same could be done for living humans today. What if we examined the hair of a modern Korean? Koreans would likely be wheat—or maybe even corn, as Pollan notes that corn lies at the root of much of the modern food chain. Koreans enjoy noodles and bread, though noodles remain popular across Korea, China, and Japan, giving them a pan-Asian vibe, while bread feels distinctly Western.

In Korea, bread has yet to reach the status of a staple food, something evident from its price. Staples are usually inexpensive, after all. In Europe or the U.S., bread is relatively cheap. Still, in Korea, the bread cost at local franchise bakeries like Paris Baguette or Tous les Jours often exceeds the government's official inflation metrics. Independent bakeries, run by young artisans, also charge comparable prices. The trendsetting bakery 'London Bagel Museum,' which has sparked a nationwide craze, sells bagels at nearly double the standard price.

Korea has a traditional rice-based food that serves as an alternative to bread.: Tteok (rice cakes). Tteok, the primary ingredient in tteokbokki (a popular street food), comes in many varieties and can serve as a filling meal. However, tteok has one major drawback: it hardens quickly, making it difficult to store for a long time. As a result, small bakeries are proliferating across neighborhoods, while traditional tteok shops are on the decline, and tteok has become more of an "event food," enjoyed mainly on big holidays and special occasions like weddings.

There is a hidden reason behind the rise of large bakery cafés in suburban areas. Many young people like to go out to the suburbs on weekends. They often stop by spacious and stylish bakery cafés to enjoy some sweet treats and snap photos for social media. However, the real driver behind this large bakery café trend is not the customers. In Korea, parents who pass property to their children face a 30% tax on the transfer. However, significant tax breaks apply if parents transfer ownership of a small family business. Regular coffee shops do not qualify, but bakery cafés do since they fall under the confectionery industry. Initially, this tax incentive was meant to support family business succession by reducing inheritance and gift tax burdens for small businesses. However, large bakery cafés have started using this policy to their advantage.

PC Bang

Young people in Korea are big fans of PC gaming. High-quality gaming requires high-spec PCs, which can be expensive at home (few parents are thrilled about kids gaming all day). So, many people go to PC Bangs, a unique internet café set up for gaming. They are affordable, and lagging is rarely an issue since they are equipped with high-performance PCs. The keyboards are flashy, and the ergonomic gaming chairs and headsets make staying focused for long sessions easy. These days, PC Bangs are almost like mini-restaurants—you can order everything from ramen to rice bowls, fried chicken, and pizza. With competition fierce, food has become a significant selling point, making up over half of PC Bang's revenue.

PC Bangs started popping up in the late 1990s, spurred on by one game: Blizzard's StarCraft. This era also saw the rollout of high-speed internet in Korea. While StarCraft itself was a hit, the ability to play against others online through Battle.net truly ignited its popularity. I remember going to a PC Bang one night with a friend who wanted to teach me StarCraft—we got so caught up in the game that I did not get home until morning! The StarCraft craze was so intense that it launched the profession of "pro gamers" and paved the way for e-sports tournaments and game broadcasting. Without those early PC Bangs and StarCraft, today's League of Legends World Championship, or The G.O.A.T. Faker, might never have come about.

Gaming has become an essential part of student life. Not all students go to PC Bangs, but almost everyone plays games on their phones. Parents might feel resigned to this reality, as it is nearly impossible to avoid games once kids have smartphones. While some apps let parents limit game time when kids are young, this control fades as they get older. But for me, there is an even more significant concern than games. At least games have clear beginnings and endings; short-form videos are another story. They provide endless, intense stimulation without boundaries, and who can trust the algorithms behind them? I worry deeply about these short-form videos' impact on kids whose sense of self is still developing.

Convenience store

I found an interesting article about convenience stores in the summer of 2024. Lately, I have noticed a lot of convenience stores popping up in my neighborhood. Still, I just realized how many there really are. According to an article from Digital Times in July 2024, the number of convenience stores in Korea surpassed that of Japan, where convenience stores originated. As of the end of 2023, the number of convenience stores in Korea exceeded 55,200, meaning there is one store for every 950 people, a number higher than the number of McDonald's locations worldwide. CNN attributed the rapid growth of convenience stores in Korea to the increase in single-person households and the concentration of the population in cities. Unlike large families, single-person households prefer the convenience of stores like these or ordering online.

Convenience stores do not just sell products; they offer various services. You can pay your bills, such as taxes and electricity fees, send domestic and international parcels, and even use pickup services for single-person households. Some stores have self-service kiosks where you can print and scan documents.

Convenience stores are very trend-sensitive. In Korea, local chains like CU and GS25 compete for the top spot, with the international chain 7-Eleven trailing closely behind. To attract customers, stores need to differentiate themselves. One of the excellent ways to do this is through collaborations with famous chefs from cooking shows. For example, CU quickly launched a "chestnut tiramisu" created by the winner of Netflix's *Culinary Class Wars*, Chef Napoli Matfia. GS25 has also released a range of products, collaborating with other famous chefs on the show.

Convenience stores, which used to be considered an urban feature, can now be found even in rural areas. These stores serve dual roles, functioning as rest stops along small highways and as neighborhood shops. Of course, rural convenience stores get fewer customers than their urban counterparts, so many are not open 24 hours.

The increase in convenience stores is partly due to the growing demand from single-person households. Another reason is the number of retirees who, feeling insecure about their financial future, decide to open their convenience stores. The average retirement age in Korea is in the early 50s, and around 70-80% of household assets are tied up in real estate. So, many early retirees, in need of income for their later years, turn to self-employment, such as opening a convenience store or a fried chicken shop. However, operating a convenience store that runs 24 hours a day is difficult alone, so they often need to hire part-time workers. With the minimum wage rising significantly, little profit is left after deducting wages for part-time staff, making it a tricky business to sustain. Sadly, despite knowing these realities, retirees are left with few other job options and feel forced into opening convenience stores.

Market

I remember the small market in my hometown where my mom used to take me as a child. That market left a lasting impression on me with its variety of scents. At the entrance, the warm smell of fresh street snacks welcomed us. Further in, the fruity scent of ripe plums, a signal that summer had arrived, wafted from the stalls of older women selling produce. The nutty aroma of sesame oil and a hint of chili powder filled the air near the oil shop. Before the fish vendor, the wet ground carried a distinct, salty fish scent. Inside the shoe store, the rubbery smell of new sneakers was unmistakable. Even now, I imagine that market waiting to welcome kids holding their parents' hands, with all those familiar scents filling the air.

But times have changed. These days, few city parents visit the market. Instead, they shop at large, scentless supermarkets or order online. With fewer families visiting, the word "traditional" has now been added to these markets, as if marking them with a sense of nostalgia. The government has tried to support these markets by requiring big supermarkets to close on the second and fourth Sundays of each month, but the effect seems limited. Some local governments have even shifted these required closures to weekdays rather than weekends, which has proven more popular.

While big supermarkets easily overshadow traditional markets, they struggle to keep up with the rise of online shopping and e-commerce. We now live in a world where two taps—"Buy" and "Pay"—bring items to our doorstep the following day. According to an article from Business.com, Korea ranks fifth in the world for e-commerce, following China, the U.S., the U.K., and Japan. Unlike the West, where Amazon dominates, Korea's e-commerce market is fiercely competitive. Coupang, like Amazon, Korea's leading search engine Naver with Naver Shopping, and several retail giants all battle for market share. So far, Amazon remains hesitant to enter this highly competitive Korean market. Coupang appears likely to dominate this market in the long term due to its significant investments in logistics centers. If that happens, the concept of *price comparison* might disappear altogether.

Public bike-sharing service

Seoul offers a cheap and convenient public bike-sharing service inspired by Paris's Vélib. The service, called "Ddareungi," is named after the sound of a bicycle bell. Using it is simple: purchase a pass through the dedicated app, scan the bike's QR code with your smartphone, and you're ready to ride. When you're done, lock the bike near any station, and it's considered returned. Unlike some systems abroad where a docking station must have an open slot, Ddareungi allows users to return bikes by locking them near the station, regardless of docking space. As of 2021, the average distance between stations was about 300 meters, and the number of stations has only grown since then, making them even more accessible. Suppose you can't find a station near your destination. In that case, it might just mean you've chosen an extremely unpopular spot—so maybe rethink going there altogether.

The popularity of shared bikes has had some unintended side effects. Bicycle shops, once a common sight in the city, are disappearing. While shared bikes might seem like a replacement for owning a bicycle, that's not entirely true. For families with kids, buying multiple bikes over the years to match a growing child's needs is inevitable. Although there are some shared bikes for children, they are very limited in number and don't meet the everyday needs of most kids. As a result, when parents need to replace or repair a child's bike, they're often forced to travel farther and farther to find a shop—a growing inconvenience.

Gas station

When I rented a car for a trip around the U.S. in 2013, one of the things that made me nervous was the gas stations. I had heard that in America, drivers pump their gas, and at the time, I had never even touched a gas pump. In Korea, gas station attendants traditionally handle everything—from filling up my tank to processing my payment. When I first touched a gas pump in the U.S., I never imagined doing the same in Korea one day. However, with rising labor costs, including minimum wage increases and mandatory holiday pay, most gas stations in Korea have now switched to self-service. These self-service stations save on labor costs and offer slightly cheaper fuel than full-service stations. Still, it's not always clear to consumers that these savings come from reduced labor costs, as fuel prices fluctuate with oil prices. Instead, it's clear that the days when consumers could simply roll down their windows to get gas are gone forever.

Despite not producing a single drop of oil, Korea generates significant revenue from it. As one of the world's most resource-poor countries, Korea imports all its crude oil, primarily from the Middle East, and imports far more than it consumes domestically. According to Korea National Oil Corporation statistics, Korea imported approximately 1 billion barrels of crude oil in 2023, ranking as the fourth-largest importer globally. Why so much oil? Korean refineries process the imported crude into products like diesel, gasoline, and jet fuel, which they then export for profit. While refining margins fluctuate with oil prices, Korean refineries typically turn a profit if the margin exceeds $5 per barrel. In 2023, Korea exported about 500 million barrels of refined petroleum products, essentially re-exporting half the imported crude.

Mobile phone store

In Korea, people typically upgrade their phones with a 2-year contract. Although direct plans, which involve purchasing a phone outright and signing up for a carrier plan online, are about 30% cheaper with no contract period, they aren't trendy. Instead, many people still visit physical mobile phone stores to get a new device. These stores are usually either local branches of major carriers or independent shops where you can choose from multiple carriers. Korea's three major carriers are KT, SK Telecom, and LG Uplus.

Buying a phone in Korea is more complicated than purchasing a SIM card for your old device. The glass windows of mobile phone stores are often plastered with ads suggesting you can get the latest phones for free. Inside, sales staff present a dizzying array of phones, plans, contract terms, discounts, and promotional gifts. For example, they may offer discounts if you sign up for a new credit card and spend a certain amount monthly or push expensive plans for the first six months in exchange for an additional discount. After 30 minutes of listening to their explanations, you may lose your way and unwittingly agree to their recommendations. It's not uncommon to leave the store with a new phone you hadn't planned on buying and to question later whether you made the right choice.

Most people sign a two-year contract with a carrier and purchase their phones on an installment plan. The monthly telecom bills are costly. If you opt for an unlimited data plan, your monthly bill will likely exceed $80. Due to rising telecom costs, more people are switching to LTE (4G) plans, which are slightly cheaper than 5G.

One app dominates Korean smartphones: KakaoTalk, often called "KaTalk." Launched in 2010, KaTalk gained massive popularity by offering free messaging at a time when carriers charged for SMS. It quickly became a must-have app for Koreans. Early in the smartphone era, no one realized that capturing the messaging market early could lead to near-monopoly dominance. Since people have little reason to use multiple messaging apps with the same contacts, users naturally gravitated toward the most widely used one. LINE Messenger, launched by Naver (Korea's leading search engine), couldn't compete domestically with KaTalk's head start and eventually shifted its focus overseas.

The company behind KaTalk, Kakao, grew into one of Korea's most successful tech firms in the smartphone era. Today, it operates in diverse sectors, including banking, securities, mobile payment services, ride-hailing, and entertainment, solidifying its position as a major conglomerate.

Subway

Finding a public restroom in the heart of Paris can be a real challenge. This might have improved recently with the Olympics, but it's hard to say. Do you know the feeling of a parent when their child says they need to use the restroom, and they have no idea where to find one? While parents living in Paris likely know where to go, visiting parents often break into a cold sweat. Nearby public facilities like the Paris subway seem like a solution, but the ticket gates block the way, and there isn't a restroom inside either. This starkly contrasts Seoul, where almost every subway station has restrooms. Most are located outside the ticket gates, serving as de facto public toilets, and are generally exceptionally clean. In

Seoul, as long as you're near a subway station, there's no need to ask kids to hold on a little longer.

Do you remember the days before smartphones, when subway passengers used to sit facing one another? We'd sneak glances at each other, pretending not to notice. We used to look at one another, but today, on the Seoul subway, everyone's head is down and glued to their screens. The only exceptions are people glancing up briefly to check their location or those resting their eyes. With so few people looking up, even the once-colorful advertisements decorating subway cars have largely disappeared.

Although Korea grapples with a severely low birth rate, societal awareness of the issue still needs to be improved. Pink seats for pregnant women have been designated on subway trains to encourage childbirth. However, respect for pregnant women appears insufficient. It's not uncommon to see elderly passengers or middle-aged women occupying them. Even when others glare at them, they remain unmoved, possibly thinking, "What makes pregnant women so special?" This often leaves pregnant women hesitant to ask for a seat, fearing conflict. Ironically, such experiences might only discourage people from having children further.

Apartment

Korea is often called the "Republic of Apartments."

If you drive along the Han River or look out over Seoul from a high vantage point, you'll be struck by the forest of apartment buildings filling the city. Why are there so many apartments in Korea? During the country's rapid industrialization, people flocked to cities for jobs, leading to overcrowding and a housing shortage. To address this, the government prioritized the construction of apartments.

While apartments lack the charm or individuality of a house, they offer convenience for workers who toiled day and night. Living in a home (single-family dwelling) meant dealing with water, sewage, electricity, and heating systems on your own—and the time and cost of repairs could add up quickly. In contrast, apartments, such as shared housing, provide these services at a lower price, making them ideal for busy urbanites. Children who grew up in apartments also tend to stick with them as adults. They never saw their parents fixing leaky pipes or broken windows, so maintaining a house feels daunting.

Apartments in Korea have evolved beyond simple living spaces; they've become the most reliable investment vehicle and a key marker of social class. The primary reason for their popularity is their seemingly unstoppable price growth. Real estate in Korea, led by apartments, has consistently risen over time, aside from a few crises. Korea's unique *jeonse* rental system—where tenants pay a lump-sum deposit often exceeding 50% of the home's value—has also fueled speculative demand for apartments. Ever heard of Psy's "Gangnam Style"? Gangnam is the most expensive area for apartments. In Korea, the wealthy own apartments in Gangnam, the middle class owns apartments elsewhere in Seoul, and the lower-income population often lives in houses.

Buying a new apartment in Korea requires both luck and patience. Most new apartments are sold through a pre-sale system, meaning developers sell units before construction begins, using the proceeds to fund the building process. Buyers apply for these units after seeing model homes or promotional materials. Suppose the pre-sale price is lower than the market value, and the location is desirable. In that case, competition is fierce, and securing a unit requires a stroke of luck. With the pre-sale system, buyers can spread the high cost of an apartment over about two years, reducing their financial burden, while developers can save costs by using buyers' money to fund the construction. However, this system has its downsides. Buyers can't inspect their homes before purchasing, leading to disappointment over construction defects once the building is completed. Some blame increasing defects on a shortage of skilled labor in the construction industry, as younger generations increasingly avoid manual labor.

One downside of apartment living is the proximity to neighbors, separated only by a wall. This wasn't an issue back when neighbors shared a sense of community. The 2015 tvN drama *Reply 1988* beautifully portrayed the warm relationships of neighbors in a small alleyway. Even apartment residents back then would treat shared hallways like village streets, freely visiting one another. However, as apartment units became larger and hallways disappeared, the environment grew more closed off. Interest in neighbors dwindled, and the sounds of daily life from next door became unwelcome noise. These days, disputes over noise between floors have become common—and sometimes escalate to severe conflicts or even crimes.

Hospital

In Korea, access to hospitals is relatively good. The country has had a national health insurance system for a long time, making medical costs generally affordable. For minor illnesses like the common cold, consultation fees rarely exceed 5,000 KRW (about $4). Recently, a system was introduced where individuals can get a refund if their annual medical expenses exceed a certain cap based on their income level. Korea doesn't have a primary care physician system, so if you're sick, you can visit any local clinic or large general hospital at your convenience. Local clinics usually don't even require appointments.

However, easy and cheap hospital access isn't always good. People tend to visit the doctor for even minor symptoms and rely heavily on medication. This has led to widespread misuse of antibiotics, raising concerns about antibiotic resistance.

In addition to Western medicine, Korea has many clinics called "hanuiwon" that practice traditional Korean medicine. Compared to general hospitals, these clinics and dental offices offer fewer treatments covered by health insurance, making their services relatively expensive.

Like Western countries, Korea has implemented the separation of prescribing and dispensing drugs. While over-the-counter medicines like cold remedies can be bought directly at pharmacies, most medications require a prescription from a doctor. Interestingly, even over-the-counter drugs can sometimes be purchased at a lower cost if bought with a prescription, as health insurance may partially cover the cost.

Korea places great emphasis on appearance. Many believe that looks are crucial to dating and career success. As a result, both men and women frequently visit dermatology clinics, and cosmetic surgery is prevalent among women. At one point, the term "Gangnam beauty" became widely used. It refers to the trend of women who undergo cosmetic surgery at the many clinics concentrated in Seoul's Gangnam district, resulting in a somewhat uniform appearance. The popularity of dermatological treatments and cosmetic surgery has drawn many doctors to these lucrative fields, creating a shortage of specialists in life-saving disciplines like emergency medicine or surgery. This imbalance has fueled ongoing disputes between the government, which seeks to expand medical school admissions, and doctors opposing the move. As of 2024, these tensions have culminated in a medical crisis.

Although Korea has a national health insurance system, many people subscribe to multiple private insurance plans. National health insurance is mandatory for all citizens and is divided into employee and regional insurance. Employees have their insurance premiums automatically deducted from their salaries at a rate of

3.5%. Regional insurance premiums are calculated based on both income and assets. Additionally, many companies provide supplementary insurance as part of their employee benefits. This coverage is sufficient for most to handle typical medical expenses, but people still opt for additional insurance plans. Some do so out of fear, while insurance companies aggressively market policies, often leveraging scenarios of potential crises. Certain companies even advertise that a cancer diagnosis could result in substantial payouts, framing it as a financial opportunity.

Doctors are among the highest-earning professionals in Korea, and the country's top students often aim to enter medical school. Some parents, disregarding their child's abilities or interests, push them relentlessly toward a medical career, subjecting them to immense pressure from a young age. There's even a saying that some students start preparing for medical school as early as elementary school. While chasing wealth in a capitalist society isn't inherently wrong, doctors don't contribute to societal progress or innovation in the same way engineers or scientists might. They don't create jobs, either. This trend of top-performing students focusing solely on medicine raises concerns about Korean society's long-term balance and development.

Veterinary clinic

Pets have become an integral part of our daily lives. Near my home, there's a small, beautiful park where I enjoy evening walks. The park features a circular grassy plaza in the center, illuminated by large LED lights that make it feel like a stage, surrounded by trees that act as a natural fence. The park is alive with people enjoying various activities—strolling, playing basketball, cycling, families playing badminton, couples with strollers, and individuals watching YouTube on benches. However, the most eye-catching presence in the park is the dogs out for their walks. They dart around joyfully, clearly the happiest beings in the park. According to Korea's 2020 Census, 15% of households had pets. Now that the COVID-19 pandemic has passed, it's likely that even more families are living with pets.

As more people own pets, veterinary clinics have become increasingly common. Some operate 24/7, while others advertise high-tech diagnostic equipment like MRI and CT scanners. These advanced services and after-hours care inevitably lead to high costs. Since pets are considered part of the family, many owners are willing to spend generously on their health. Still, an increasing number of pet owners are turning to pet insurance to save on medical bills. Monthly premiums range from 40,000 to 90,000 KRW (about $30-70), which isn't particularly cheap compared to human health insurance.

Bank

Cash has almost disappeared in daily life. The 50,000 KRW bill I keep in my cardholder for emergencies has been untouched for three months. In Korea, credit and debit cards, mobile payment services, and bank transfers have become so widespread that there's little need to carry cash. Coins are even rarer. Reflecting this trend, many stores no longer accept cash, and buses are starting to follow suit. For credit cards, inserting the card into a terminal for chip-based payments (IC cards) is the norm. While contactless credit cards are quietly gaining traction, they have yet to be widely adopted due to limited promotion and a lack of compatible terminals. Apple Pay made a late entry into Korea, but its adoption is hindered by the slow rollout of NFC-enabled terminals and the lack of a transit card feature. Meanwhile, Samsung has created a virtually cashless environment in Korea with Samsung Pay integrated into its smartphones. Meanwhile, Samsung has created a virtually cashless world with Samsung Pay. Credit card companies, wary of disrupting their relationship with Samsung, which offers Samsung Pay for free, have been hesitant to expand support for Apple Pay.

Though cash is mainly unnecessary, there are still occasions where it is preferred. Weddings and funerals are two instances where giving cash is customary as a gesture of respect. When unable to attend in person, people often transfer money to a friend, asking them to deliver it in cash. However, direct bank transfers for such events have become more common since the pandemic. During family gatherings on traditional holidays, money is often used for gifting. It feels more personal and meaningful to hand over physical cash to parents or nieces and nephews than making a bank transfer.

As most banking needs can now be handled through mobile banking, local bank branches are gradually disappearing. Younger generations, who rarely visit banks, are largely unaffected by this trend. However, older adults less familiar with smartphones often find the loss of nearby branches a significant inconvenience. We may soon see bank service hubs, like mobile phone stores offering multiple carriers, where services from various banks are combined in one location.

Bank counters may be less crowded, but waiting times have grown longer. This is because the customers who visit branches often require more complex assistance. Another contributing factor is stricter regulations on financial investment products, which mandate that banks thoroughly explain these products to customers and confirm their understanding before proceeding.

This shift also ties into a broader economic context. As Korea enters an era of low growth and interest rates, banks have seen their profit margins shrink. They've ramped up sales of non-deposit investment products to make up for reduced interest income. However, this has occasionally led to issues, as banks sometimes push complex financial products to customers with limited financial knowledge, creating significant social problems. I remember the Financial Supervisory Service building near my workplace, where protests over the mis-selling of financial products were a constant sight. As a result, completing financial investment transactions at banks now takes significantly more time.

Koreans, in general, need more financial literacy. Schools focus heavily on core subjects like Korean, English, and math but offer little education about money management. This knowledge gap leads to reckless investments and frequent financial scams. Scammers often lure people in by claiming to share some exclusive, confidential information just with them. People who lack financial knowledge and are driven by greed may fail to grasp the true meaning behind those words: You are my prey. Without adequate education on earning, investing, and managing money, people often pay a steep price for learning these lessons the hard way. The flow of capital—where money enters the stock market, helps companies grow and generates returns for investors—has yet to take root in Korea. Although the government introduced a retirement pension system similar to the U.S. 401(k) in 2012, much of this money remains in low-interest bank products instead of being funneled into the capital markets. Koreans' strong preference for real estate investments is another reason capital often fails to create value in the broader economy.

Movie theater

The 21st century has brought significant changes to

the movie theater experience. As sizeable corporate capital entered the film industry, small, unique theaters with distinct personalities disappeared, giving way to sleek, modern multiplexes. Today, three major companies—CGV, Lotte Cinema, and Megabox—dominate the Korean movie theater market. The pandemic hit theaters hard, and ticket prices in response have risen to a burdensome level. As of 2024, a movie ticket costs 15,000 KRW. While high prices might be tolerable if exciting new films were regularly released, the unfortunate reality is that the film industry is in a slump. As a result, theaters now resort to re-screening old box office hits or showing alternative content like musicals and concerts. It feels as though the era of going to theaters to watch movies is nearing its end.

The rise of streaming giants like Netflix has cast an even darker shadow over Korean cinema and theaters. A Korean proverb says, "*The bear does the tricks, but someone else takes the money.*" While Netflix has substantially invested in Korea's film industry, it retains all the rights. As a result, even when a movie or drama succeeds, creators often end up with little to show for their efforts. Watching the massive global success of *Squid Game* while its creators earned relatively little left me feeling bitter about how Korea's film industry seems to have become a subcontractor for Netflix. Even Hwang Dong-hyuk, the director of *Squid Game*, admitted in an interview that financial considerations were among the reasons he decided to make a second season.

In Korea, celebrities are held to an extraordinarily

high standard of morality. Public scrutiny becomes even more intense when someone gains popularity with a good image. You might recall classmates who stood out for their creative flair or artistic talents — those qualities are often innate. These are the types of people who grow up to become entertainers. Their natural flair is hard to contain; it fuels incredible movies and dramas but can also create chaos in their personal lives.

However, while the Korean public idolizes their professional talent, they are unwilling to accept their imperfections. The belief that influential celebrities must also be moral role models stems from propaganda dating back to Korea's military dictatorship era.

My favorite drama is *My Mister*, which aired on tvN in 2018. This drama, praised by novelist Paulo Coelho as "a flawless description of the human condition," left a deep impression on viewers. One of its lead actors, Lee Sun-kyun, moved audiences with his performance. Tragically, in the winter of 2023, Lee became the target of a frenzied media witch hunt over his personal life, ultimately leading him to end his own life.

Optical shop

Since videos have taken over our brains, our eyes rarely get a break. We constantly pull out our phones to watch videos. We don't focus on our food while eating, overlook obstacles on the streets while walking, and neglect to power down our sympathetic nervous system before bed. In Korea, presbyopia (age-related farsightedness) typically starts in one's 50s, but observing my peers, it appears as early as the mid-40s. People now rely on supplements like lutein and zeaxanthin to support eye health, much like taking hangover cures before drinking, while continuing their video consumption habits. With this trend, they'll likely visit optical shops earlier than previous generations.

Waiting a week to get a new pair of glasses sounds utterly foreign to someone like me who has lived in Korea all my life. Here, you can get a new pair of glasses on the spot, and even for specialized lenses, it usually takes just a day or two. Eye exams are provided free of charge at optical shops. However, I suspect the cost is already factored into the price of frames and lenses. Frame prices typically range from 50,000 to 100,000 KRW, though designer brands can vary significantly. Unless they specialize in presbyopia or severe vision correction, lens prices are usually similar to frame prices and not overly expensive. Additionally, salaried workers can include eyewear expenses in the medical deductions category during annual tax filings, potentially reducing their taxes.

Wedding hall

Preparing for a wedding is long and complex, but the ceremony is short and straightforward. The actual wedding event lasts about 30 minutes, and with the meal included, it's roughly a three-hour affair. Most weddings occur in specialized halls or hotels, typically reserved six months to a year in advance. As food is taken very seriously in Korean culture, the quality of the meal is a critical factor when choosing a wedding venue. In the past, the bride or groom often invited a respected figure to give a congratulatory speech. Still, nowadays, it's more common for the parents of both families to take on this role. There is also a growing emphasis on the wedding performance or celebratory songs. Guests typically celebrate by giving cash, while close friends might give additional presents. Cash gifts function as a reciprocal fund; people often feel slighted if they don't receive as much as they've given in the past. Most couples leave for their honeymoon on the wedding day or the next day, and it's rare for them to postpone their trip.

Marriage is undoubtedly a personal choice, but in Korea, children preparing for marriage often feel considerable pressure to please their parents. Korean society remains somewhat patriarchal, and there's still a lingering notion that children are the property of their parents. At the same time, it's not uncommon for children to rely on their parents for housing costs, as purchasing a home is prohibitively expensive for young professionals. We refer to the children of wealthy parents as "gold spoons" and those from less fortunate families as "dirt spoons." In the 2024 hit Netflix cooking show *Culinary Class Wars*, chefs were humorously classified as "White Spoon" or "Black Spoon," likely parodying this concept. For "gold spoon" children, marriage often requires parental approval, as wealthy parents tend to view their child's marriage as a kind of business decision. While Cinderella-style dramas featuring marriages between the rich and the less fortunate abound, people generally prefer to marry someone from a similar financial background.

Police station

How often does one visit a police station in their lifetime? I've never been lucky enough to set foot in one and never heard of any friends going. My only knowledge of police stations comes from TV shows and movies. In Korea, pickpocketing has become nearly obsolete, and theft cases have visibly decreased thanks to the widespread use of CCTV. Since private firearm ownership is prohibited, gun-related incidents are mostly confined to the military. Women can typically walk alone late at night without much fear. Videos of young foreign YouTubers marveling at the sight of schoolgirls commuting home safely after dark may astonish viewers abroad, but for Koreans, it's hardly surprising. A seemingly safe environment doesn't mean there's no crime. Crimes like voice phishing targeting older adults, digital sex crimes, random acts of violence against the public, and brutal murders have been on the rise.

The police in Korea are generally seen as approachable rather than authoritarian or intimidating. But this friendly image didn't develop overnight. There was a time when Korean police indiscriminately wielded "batons" against civilians. Up until the 1980s, Korea was under military rule, and the police served as enforcers for the regime, often instilling fear and exercising unchecked authority. Widespread police violence and corruption left many innocent citizens victimized. However, through the people's relentless fight for democracy, the military government was ousted, which led to a significant transformation of the police into a more restrained and accountable institution.

However, unlike the democratized police force, there remains an organization that has yet to be democratized: the prosecution. The prosecution seems stuck in the 1980s under a military regime, failing to adapt to the changes of the times. Although it is not the military, the prosecution emphasizes hierarchy excessively, making it difficult for conscientious voices to emerge from within. The real issue lies in the prosecution's abuse of its prosecutorial power to suit its own interests. To be precise, it often sides with those in power, shamelessly engaging in unfair practices.

Under the current president, who is a former prosecutor, the prosecution has turned a blind eye to allegations of various crimes and government interference involving the First Lady. As a result, many Koreans are calling for justice. If this ongoing conflict is resolved in a way that aligns with the people's expectations, I believe it will mark a significant step forward for democracy in Korea.

Bookstore

It's not just trendy spots that have changed over time. While the Hongdae district excites today's youth, 30 years ago, Jongno was what Hongdae is now. Jongno, located between Gwanghwamun and Dongdaemun, was the go-to area for young people, and large bookstores were a prominent feature of the neighborhood. These bookstores often served as popular meeting points. Back then, if you arrived early for a meeting, you'd step into a bookstore to browse through books while waiting. Today, most people spend their time on YouTube or gaming apps. Although the same bookstores still stand in Jongno, the readers who once filled them are long gone. This trend is reflected in reading statistics: according to a 2021 government survey, only 47.5% of adults in Korea had read at least one book in the past year, marking a drop of 8.2 percentage points from the previous year. In other words, over half of the population doesn't read even a single book annually. It's a sobering thought that books are losing out to YouTube and video games.

Will there come a time when people revisit bookstores to buy bestsellers and rediscover the joy of holding a book in their hands? In 2024, the Nobel Prize in Literature was awarded to Han Kang, a Korean female author. Her books flew off the shelves, and printing presses worked non-stop to meet the sudden demand. While the publishing industry hopes this signals a revival of reading culture, it's hard to believe that even the glory of a Nobel Prize can lure people back from the addictive pull of video content.

These days, we access information so quickly and effortlessly. The internet and YouTube do remarkably well in delivering what we need. However, because the effort we put in is minimal, the information we gain often slips away just as quickly. Books, on the other hand, offer a contrasting experience. Reading a book is undeniably slower and more demanding, but the knowledge we gain tends to stay with us longer. Furthermore, books often introduce us to unexpected insights and serendipitous discoveries, leading us to new paths. While YouTube's algorithm occasionally recommends excellent videos, these moments are fleeting, drowned out by the endless stream of other videos queued up below.

Factory

Factories once drew people into cities but have since quietly disappeared. During the height of industrialization, factories began popping up in urban areas. Light industries, which required significant manual labor, found cities ideal due to their ready supply of workers. People who found jobs in urban factories encouraged their families and friends from rural areas to join them, leading to a mass migration into cities. As cities grew, the once-bustling factories gradually became relics. While the factory buildings often remained, their operations moved to suburban areas, rural regions, or overseas. Over time, cities transformed into modern residential and commercial hubs, and people began to see old factories as out of place. However, younger generations, drawn to the unconventional charm, saw the outdated structures as trendy. They repurposed the exteriors of these old factories into hip cultural spaces. Seoul's Seongsu-dong, once known for its handmade shoe factories, has become a prime example of this transformation and is now a hotspot for young people.

While urban factories have been reimagined as cultural spaces, factories outside the city are often overlooked and abandoned as workplaces. The older generation, born in a poorer era, worked tirelessly in factories or any job available to escape poverty. In contrast, the younger generation, born into relative wealth, tends to shy away from physical labor. As a result, it's increasingly rare to see young Koreans working in the factories that remain in Korea.

Factories have had no choice but to rely on foreign workers. Many companies moved their production facilities overseas to benefit from cheaper labor. Foreign labor has become essential for small and medium-sized businesses still operating in Korea. According to government data released in October 2024, as of the end of 2023, approximately 2.46 million foreigners lived in Korea for three months or longer, an increase of 200,000 compared to 2022. The rise in foreign workers was the main contributor to this growth. These workers are essential not only to factories but also to farms and fishing communities. It's often said that Korean agricultural products wouldn't make it to our dining tables without foreign labor.

Gym

Trends paint the city in new colors. Walking down the street, you will likely be handed flyers advertising newly opened gyms. Look up, and you'll see gyms filling floors in countless buildings. While people used to exercise primarily to lose weight, today's gym-goers are more focused on building strong and healthy bodies. The societal emphasis on work-life balance has also driven many to spend their post-work hours at the gym or Pilates studios. According to a September 2024 survey by HR company Incruit, 7 out of 10 office workers exercise for self-care and to improve their physical fitness. The most popular activities were gym workouts, walking, running, Pilates, and yoga.

The body has become a means of expressing one's desires. While many people still flaunt material possessions like cars and handbags on social media, there's been a noticeable rise in individuals showcasing their fit, healthy physiques. It's now common to see people who have sculpted their bodies sharing professional body profile photos. With this growing fitness trend, shows like Channel A's *The Iron Squad* and Netflix's *Physical: 100* have gained massive popularity. Gyms are so crowded that trendsetters have moved off the gym treadmills and onto the spacious paths along the

Han River. Naturally, crowds have followed. These days, running in groups is even more fashionable than running alone. However, some running crews have drawn criticism for inconveniencing others, such as blocking narrow streets or pausing mid-run to take group photos.

One of the runners I've seen stands out vividly in my memory. In 2017, I took a road trip through Norway. While driving along Route 604, which leads deep into the Nigardsbreen glacier, I noticed no houses, cars, or signs of civilization—just the serene jade-green river flowing nearby. As I drove further, I spotted a young woman running alone on this lonely stretch of road. I couldn't help but wonder: why was she running here, alone, in the middle of nowhere on a sunny afternoon? It was clear she wasn't running to impress anyone.

<u>2</u>
What We Eat

Korea's unique cuisine and resilience

Koreans have developed a diverse cuisine despite harsh natural conditions and war history. Korea is a mountainous country, which means there is limited farmland for growing rice. On top of this, Korea has endured numerous invasions over the centuries, leading to frequent famine. How, then, did Koreans manage to survive hunger and malnutrition? They turned to the mountains for solutions. The mountains are rich in wild plants, and through trial and error, Koreans identified which ones were edible, nutritious, and flavorful. These edible wild plants, known as "namul," became a staple. Namul dishes are not only tasty but also rich in vitamins and minerals. When dried, they make excellent preserved foods. According to the Korea Heritage Agency, there are over 450 varieties of namul. One well-known example is bracken fern (Gosari in Korean), which is said to be eaten exclusively by Koreans worldwide. While raw bracken is toxic, the poison is removed through boiling and repeated soaking.

Italy, famous for its culinary variety, has a similar story. John Hooper says in his book *The Italians*: "Frequent wars and social conflicts often led to widespread hunger, which significantly contributed to the wide range of Italian food. For example, the arugula salad, which only became popular in the English-speaking world in the 1990s, has roots in Italy during and after World War II, when Italians searched for edible wild plants to survive."

Kimchi

For Koreans, kimchi is more than just food; it is a cultural tradition. Kimchi is made by seasoning salted cabbage with chili powder and fermenting it. While cabbage kimchi is the most well-known, dozens of types are made from various vegetables like radishes, cucumbers, and green onions. Thanks to the salt preservation of cabbage, cabbage kimchi lasts a long time, making it an ideal food for storage. It was especially essential during winter when fresh produce was hard to find. As winter approaches, Korean families gather to prepare enough kimchi to last through the season, a practice known as "gimjang." It is similar to the Italian tradition of making tomato passata once a year.

Kimchi varies by region, as people add locally available ingredients, and each household often has its family recipe passed down through generations. Families make kimchi together and then share it among themselves to take home. Nearly every Korean household has a special refrigerator that stores kimchi, which helps keep the flavor stable year-round by precisely regulating temperature.

I visit my in-laws' rural home every year to help make kimchi. My mother-in-law preps a day in advance by soaking napa cabbage in salted water and preparing the seasoning mixture. Once we arrive, we thoroughly rinse the cabbage, let it drain for about a day, and then get to work the next day, mixing the seasoning into the cabbage to make the kimchi. My in-laws add pungent *jeotgal* (salted fermented seafood) to their recipe, giving the kimchi a rich, deep flavor once fully fermented.

Home-cooked meal

Whenever I meet someone from another country, I always ask one question: "What's a typical home-cooked meal in your country?" I hope to hear, "We eat this or that type of dish every day," but I have rarely found anyone who can give a clear answer. So, what if you asked this question to a Korean? Korean home-cooked meals are standardized, so you would likely get a similar answer from anyone. A typical Korean home meal includes *bab* (steamed rice), *gug* (soup), and *banchan* (side dishes), with one or two main dishes added.

The most important part of the meal is bab. While it is steamed rice, the word for bab in Korean also means "meal" itself. So, when asking someone if they have eaten, I ask, "Have you had bab?" Cooking bab requires an electric rice cooker for about 30 minutes, so preparing bab is usually the first task when making a meal. But in 1996, CJ CheilJedang introduced a game-changing invention: instant rice, ready in just two minutes in the microwave. (The product name is Haetban.) With the cooking time reduced from thirty minutes to two, it is a fantastic convenience, commonly used when rice runs low at home or on outings like camping.

Gug (Soup) is usually a side dish but can become the main dish depending on the ingredients. A simple doenjang-gug (soybean paste soup), made with whatever is in the fridge, is often served as a side. However, if the soup includes a pricier ingredient like fish, it can take center stage as the main dish. As awareness of health risks from high salt intake has recently grown, fewer Korean meals include soup since some traditional soups are pretty salty.

One hallmark of Korean dining is the variety of banchan (side dishes) everyone shares at the table. One thing that surprises many foreign visitors to Korean restaurants is the wide assortment of complimentary side dishes. This tradition comes from how Koreans eat at home: with multiple side dishes on the table. Families make various side dishes at home in advance, store them in the fridge, and bring them out for each meal.

A meal of rice and side dishes can be simple, so the

mother often makes a main dish. This main dish is usually what the kids are curious about when asking, "What's for dinner?" It depends on what ingredients are available in the fridge—a meat dish or a stew. Incidentally, the names of Korean dishes are often a combination of the main ingredient and cooking method. For example, tteokbokki combines tteok (rice cake) and bokki (stir-fried). At the same time, kimchi jjigae is a blend of kimchi (the main ingredient) and jjigae (stew).

Meat

Pork is Korea's favorite meat, and there is a particular obsession with samgyeopsal (pork belly). Among the many cuts of pork, samgyeopsal stands out as the most popular, so much so that Korea imports it to meet demand while exporting other less popular cuts. Koreans love grilling samgyeopsal over charcoal or on a griddle. Its appeal lies in the savory aroma of pork fat caramelizing as it cooks. However, there's a fine line between delicious and overwhelming. Recently, a restaurant in Jeju Island stirred controversy for serving samgyeopsal with too much fat. The next most popular pork cut for grilling is moksal (pork neck). Other cuts, like pork ribs, are typically marinated before grilling, and loin and tenderloin are often used to make pork cutlets (tonkatsu).

Samgyeopsal pairs perfectly with soju. Before 1998, soju had an alcohol content of 25%, making it bitter and pungent and considered a man's drink. Then, in 1998, HiteJinro introduced Chamisul, a lower-alcohol soju that became a hit. This began a trend toward milder soju, which now averages around 16% alcohol. This lighter flavor has broadened soju's appeal, especially among younger women.

Korea is a chicken kingdom, with many restaurants in every neighborhood. Opening a chicken restaurant is often the go-to option for retirees with limited funds, leading to intense competition. This has resulted in a dazzling variety of chicken dishes, and you'll frequently see TV ads featuring celebrities promoting new items. Koreans prefer fried chicken, which, while possible to make at home, is most often ordered from franchise restaurants. Children love chicken, so families typically eat it about once a week. While a raw chicken costs around $5, a fried chicken meal from a major franchise can cost $20 with delivery fees, making it relatively expensive. Koreans traditionally prefer fatty parts like legs and wings, while lean breast meat is popular among fitness enthusiasts.

Chicken is also enjoyed in samgye-tang (ginseng chicken soup) and dakbokkeum-tang (spicy chicken stew). Samgye-tang is a traditional health food, often eaten to combat summer heat. There are even specific days called *boknal* dedicated to eating samgye-tang. However, this custom harks back to a time when meat was scarce and considered a luxury. Today, with meat readily available, every day could be seen as a modern-day boknal.

Cold beer pairs wonderfully with chicken; chicken restaurants often deliver draft beer alongside their food. In Korea, pale lagers are the most popular beer, though their flavor is somewhat bland. To enhance the experience, people often mix beer with soju, creating a cocktail known as *somaek*. While everyone has their preferred ratio, the golden ratio is considered 7 parts beer to 3 parts soju.

Korean beef, known as hanwoo, is both delicious and expensive. Well-marbled hanwoo sirloin is incredibly tender and flavorful. Due to its high demand and limited supply, hanwoo commands prices two to three times higher than pork in restaurants. Scandals involving mixing cheap imported beef with hanwoo occasionally made headlines in the past, but these have largely disappeared. Koreans prefer grilling hanwoo.

Because domestic production can't keep up with demand, Korea imports large quantities of beef from the U.S. and Australia. Imported beef is about half the price of hanwoo. Argentine beef is rarely seen in Korean markets despite Argentina's reputation for high-quality beef.

U.S. beef had a rocky introduction to Korea. In 2003, imports were halted due to mad cow disease. When the newly elected Lee Myung-bak administration decided to resume imports in 2008, massive protests erupted. While the demonstrations were more about opposing the conservative government than the beef itself, even political ideals can't compete with lower prices in a free-market economy. Incidentally, U.S. beef is the cheapest available in Korea. According to a 2024 report, Korea has been the largest importer of U.S. beef for three consecutive years, from 2021 to 2023.

While Koreans also eat duck and lamb, they are far less popular. Duck is usually enjoyed smoked, while lamb is most commonly served as a skewer. Recently, more restaurants have started offering grilled lamb chops, but neither can rival the dominance of pork and beef.

Seafood

Koreans are said to consume more seafood than anyone else in the world. According to a 2016 United Nations Industrial Development Organization report, Korea surpassed Norway and Japan to claim the top spot for per capita seafood consumption. It's surprising that Korea eats the most seafood, given that neighboring Japan is also known for its seafood culture, and Western countries offer plenty of fish dishes like salmon.

The likely reason is that Koreans enjoy fish and various other seafood. Koreans love fish the most but also appreciate shellfish, crab, and seaweed. Popular fish include mackerel, pollock, and squid. Mackerel is often grilled, pollock is used in soups, and squid is eaten raw as sashimi or dried as a snack. Pollock, a cold-water species, has disappeared from Korean waters due to rising sea temperatures and is now entirely imported. Koreans also enjoy raw fish, but not all fish are eaten this way. The most popular choices for sashimi are Olive flounder (gwangeo in Korean) and rockfish (ureok in Korean). After barbecue restaurants, sashimi spots are among the most popular dining establishments. Unlike some other cultures, Koreans are not fond of deep-fried fish.

When it comes to shellfish, Koreans favor clams like bajirak and oysters. Bajirak kalguksu (knife-cut noodle soup with clams) is a classic comfort dish for the everyday Korean. Oysters are farmed mainly along Korea's coastal regions. Foreign visitors are often shocked by the high price of Korean beef and equally surprised by how affordable oysters are.

Smaller seafood, like shrimp, is often fermented with salt to make jeotgal (salted fermented seafood). Jeotgal is a staple seasoning in Korean cuisine, used to flavor kimchi or neutralize the fatty smell of meats.

Ramen

If rice is the staple food of Koreans, snacks are often wheat-based, and the most iconic wheat-based snack is ramen. Loved by people of all ages, hundreds of ramen varieties are sold to cater to diverse tastes. Korean ramen is generally spicy, and people's preference for spiciness is shifting not toward milder flavors but toward extreme heat, as seen with products like Buldak Bokkeum Myeon.

Did you know that spiciness is technically a form of pain? The human body has receptors in the skin that detect temperature. However, scientists had trouble identifying them for a long time. Interestingly, these receptors also react to compounds like capsaicin (the chemical responsible for spiciness), mistaking it for heat and sending a signal to the brain. David Julius won the 2021 Nobel Prize in Physiology or Medicine for discovering the body's temperature sensors using capsaicin.

Ramen comes in two main types: packet ramen and cup ramen. While packet ramen requires more preparation, it tastes much better than its instant cup counterpart. Packet ramen requires cooking equipment and heat, making it harder to prepare in convenience stores or outdoor settings. However, with the invention of ramen-cooking machines, people can now enjoy the rich flavor of packet ramen even at convenience stores.

Recently, the Han River has become a ramen haven for foreigners. Many visit Han River parks, buy packet ramen from nearby convenience stores, cook it, and enjoy it while taking in the scenic river view. I haven't tried it myself, but it sounds like it would be delicious. Ramen's popularity has even led to the emergence of 24-hour unmanned ramen shops in the city.

Restaurant

Korean restaurants can be categorized into Korean, Chinese, Japanese, and Western cuisine. According to Statistics Korea, Korean restaurants dominate the market. However, it's easy to spot many Chinese and Japanese restaurants walking through city streets.

When traveling abroad, I rely on Google Maps to find nearby restaurants. In Korea, though, I don't use Google Maps. While Google dominates the global search engine market, Korea is an exception. Here, I use map apps created by the Korean search engine Naver or Daum to find places to eat. These apps provide quick reviews and ratings, which are usually reliable, though occasionally influenced by restaurant marketing. I also look through blogs for recommendations. While some posts are advertisements, with a discerning eye, I can find genuine reviews that pay off.

Korea has an unusually high number of restaurants. As of 2022, there were about 800,000 restaurants, equating to 1.6 restaurants per 100 people. Why so many? Many people see the restaurant business as easy, especially retirees who need more savings—many open chicken restaurants. With a limited customer base and many competitors, the restaurant industry is fiercely competitive, leading to frequent closures. This churn means interior design businesses are often the only ones profiting.

Other factors also challenge the restaurant industry. Younger generations now prefer exercise to drinking, and company drinking parties have significantly decreased. Rising labor costs burden restaurant owners, and finding staff willing to work late hours has become more challenging. For these reasons, many restaurants have maintained the shorter operating hours introduced during the COVID-19 pandemic.

Local restaurants with limited menus often post large

signs with dishes and prices on the walls. Restaurants with extensive menus may have printed menus, but outside tourist areas, English menus are rare since the primary customers are Korean, and many staff don't speak English fluently. Younger staff members can typically manage essential English communication, so there's no need to worry too much.

Due to rising labor costs and aggressive marketing by tech companies, many restaurants now have tablets at each table for ordering. These tablets often allow you to switch the language to English or other foreign languages. In food-focused restaurants, you can order and pay directly through the tablet. However, in drinking establishments, where customers order more alcohol as the night goes on, tablets are used for orders only, and payment is made at the end of the visit.

You can call a restaurant server without tablets by pressing a small buzzer at the table or simply waving them over. Spoons, chopsticks, and napkins are usually stored discreetly under the table. Water is always free in Korean restaurants. While Korean tap water is clean and low in lime, most households use water purifiers or buy bottled water. Restaurants typically serve pre-filtered water stored in refrigerated bottles. Koreans prefer cold water, so lukewarm water is rarely served.

Recently, more restaurants have started using disposable paper cups for water, contrasting with the increasingly elegant plates used for food. This change is likely brought about by the pandemic.

After your meal, payment is made at the front counter

rather than the table. Korea has no tipping culture, and taxes are included in menu prices, so no mental math is required. Nearly all restaurants accept credit cards, and most Koreans prefer card payments. While street food vendors or traditional markets may occasionally ask for cash, it's becoming a rarity. In cities, people hardly use cash anymore and have even stopped carrying wallets.

Food delivery

Food delivery has become one of the most significant changes in daily life due to COVID-19. As dining out became difficult due to social distancing, the use of food delivery apps skyrocketed. These platforms now go beyond delivering meals, extending their services to beverages like coffee and necessities. The competition between delivery platforms has intensified, leading to an increase in enticing offers like free delivery. Thanks to these platforms, I felt the world had become much more convenient until I visited a kimchi stew restaurant with my son, where we often ordered.

We ordered a 20,000 KRW combo menu, and out of curiosity, I opened the delivery app to compare prices. To my surprise, the same meal was listed for 22,000 KRW on the app—a 10% markup—and an additional 3,000 KRW delivery fee. That's when I realized that I had been paying 25% more for the convenience of delivery. I wondered if I was spending too much money to place an order and track a rider's location.

So, have restaurants profited significantly from the rise of delivery platforms? Not at all. When these platforms first emerged, they did bring in more orders, prompting many restaurants to join. However, their true ambitions surfaced once these platforms had locked consumers and producers into their ecosystem. They began arbitrarily setting commission rates, pressuring restaurants to raise menu prices, and even shifting the cost of their free delivery promotions onto the restaurants. Many restaurants are losing their margins to these platforms and increasingly becoming their captives.

The food service industry cannot grow explosively unless there's a sudden population boom or people start eating six meals daily. It's inherently a market with limited growth potential. A parasitic middleman has entered this constrained market, draining producers' profits and passing the costs onto consumers. It's a problematic situation for everyone involved.

<u>3</u>
I Am From

Koreans living on an island

Koreans live on the Korean Peninsula, located at the eastern end of the Asian continent, close to China. Historically, Korea has maintained a largely homogenous culture and language, partly because there has never been large-scale immigration from other ethnic groups. Today, the Korean Peninsula shares its northern borders with China and Russia. At the same time, the island nation of Japan lies just to the south. Korea, China, and Japan are geographically close and have influenced each other for centuries.

Koreans seem to live as if they are on an island. But isn't the Korean Peninsula attached to the continent? After World War II ended in 1945, Korea was divided into South and North. For South Koreans, this division created a physical and political barrier, isolating them from the rest of the continent. South Koreans cannot reach other countries by land since the heavily fortified border with North Korea blocks the way. The northern border is less of a boundary and more like a dead-end street they cannot cross. When traveling in Europe, where crossing borders by car is standard, Koreans living on an island often express a unique curiosity about land travel in other parts of the world.

Mountain and Sea

The Korean Peninsula has a long mountain range, known as the Taebaek Mountains, that runs along the spine of the land, primarily on the eastern side. Because of this, the terrain in Korea is higher in the east and lower in the west. The most famous mountains and ski resorts are in the east, while the west features vast plains and farmland. Among Korea's mountains, Seoraksan is the most well-known.

Korea is surrounded by seas that, while connected, are known by different names depending on their location. To the east lies the East Sea, to the west is the Yellow Sea, and to the south is the South Sea. Three seas also have distinct characteristics regarding depth, water color, and tidal patterns. The East Sea is deep, with clear water due to its sandy seabed and relatively calm tides.

The location is renowned for its stunning blue waters and beautiful sunrises.

In contrast, the Yellow Sea is shallow with a muddy seabed, causing its water to appear murky; its large tidal fluctuations, mudflats, and sunset views are iconic. I remember the first time I visited a beach along the Yellow Sea with a friend. Having only swum in the clear waters of the East Sea, I was surprised to see people splashing around in muddy water, which was a culture shock.

The South Sea combines features of the East and Yellow Seas. Overall, it is more similar to the East Sea, which has a unique charm due to its many islands of various sizes.

Territory and Forest

Korea is considered a small country in terms of land area. If neighboring China is like an elephant, Korea would be about the size of a mouse. Globally, Korea ranks 109th in land area, similar in size to Iceland, Hungary in Europe, Jordan in the Middle East, and Guatemala in Central America. Korea has been gradually expanding its territory through land reclamation projects, much like the Netherlands, but very few people notice this.

Mountains are a common sight for Koreans. Approximately 70% of Korea's land is mountainous, so you can easily see mountains no matter which city you visit. Because there are so many mountains, Koreans often associate forests with mountains. This is because forests are always found on mountains, and it is rare to see vast forests on flat land.

In 2012, while on a business trip to France, I experienced this firsthand. After a week of work, I rented a car and went on a road trip around France for a few days. On the way to the Château de Chenonceau in the central region, I came across a massive forest. I would expect to see mountains, but none were there. It was a forest on flat land. The forest was so lush and well-preserved that it quickly subdued the surrounding colors. It was a real forest I had never seen before.

More extreme climate than expected

Korea has long experienced a climate with extreme temperature swings. In July 2022, when the UK suffered from an intense heatwave, I was surprised to hear that most British homes did not have air conditioning. It is hard to imagine getting through the summer without AC in Korea. Korean summers are hot and extremely humid, with tropical nights making it difficult to sleep without air conditioning. Korea's climate also sees a dramatic temperature difference between seasons. In the summer, temperatures can soar to 104°F (40°C), while in winter, they can plunge to -4°F (-20°C). This extreme range has even led a U.S. Marine Corps commander to comment that Korea's environment is ideal for intense training exercises.

Like much of the world, Korea also feels the impact of climate change. Spring and fall are shortening, while summers are becoming longer. Along with heat waves, heavy localized downpours have become more frequent. 2024 marked the hottest summer on record in Korea. Seoul experienced 44 consecutive days of tropical nights, setting a record, and the country overall saw three times the typical number of tropical nights, which is both surprising and concerning. I hope summer 2025 does not surpass it as the hottest on record.

Population

With a population of around 50 million, Korea ranks 28th globally. Countries with similar population sizes include Italy and Spain in Europe, Colombia and Argentina in South America, Kenya and Uganda in Africa, and Myanmar in Southeast Asia. About 45% of Koreans live in the capital, Seoul, and its surrounding metro area, leading to high population density in major cities and concerns over population decline in rural areas. The average age in Korea is 44, making it hard to consider Korea a young country.

Approximately 300,000 Koreans are born each year, and about the same number pass away. However, as birth rates have steadily declined, annual births fell below 300,000 in 2020, marking a population death cross. By

2023, Korea's total fertility rate dropped to just 0.7, sparking concerns about the nation's future viability. The government has invested significant funds to tackle low birth rates, but a definitive solution remains out of reach.

The term *nuclear family* became common during Korea's rapid urbanization. Still, as younger generations marry later, *single-person households* are a frequent topic. Reflecting this trend, the TV show *I Live Alone* (a popular MBC reality program where celebrities showcase their single lifestyles) has gained immense popularity. Some politicians, however, criticized such shows as promoting single living and contributing to low birth rates. It is hard to feel confident that Korea will overcome its low birth rate crisis when faced with this level of political insight.

Language

Koreans speak a unique language that has little similarity to any other on Earth. Korean is classified as an isolating language with few connections to different language families, making learning incredibly challenging for native English speakers. The U.S. Foreign Service Institute (FSI) categorizes languages into four difficulty levels for English speakers. Korean ranks in the most difficult, Level 4. However, for many Mongolians, Korean does not seem as challenging. In recent YouTube videos featuring travel in Mongolia, many Mongolians speak Korean. While it's known that many Mongolians come to Korea for work, their rapid language acquisition is impressive. They may retain the linguistic adaptability of their nomadic ancestors.

Koreans are deeply loved and proud of their unique writing system, Hangul. If asked to name a single cultural treasure, most would choose Hangul. Korea even celebrates October 9 as Hangul Day, a national holiday. But why are Koreans so passionate about their alphabet?

While Koreans communicated in their language for centuries, they did not have a native script, relying instead on Chinese characters (Hanja). However, Hanja was difficult to learn, and literacy rates among the general public needed to be higher. In the mid-15th century, King Sejong The Great, the fourth king of the Joseon Dynasty, felt deep compassion for his people who could not read Hanja. Therefore, he created a new writing system based on the sounds of the Korean language, resulting in Hangul. Yet, this new script was not immediately adopted; the ruling elite at the time strongly preferred Hanja and even opposed the creation of Hangul, seeing no need for a new script. Their resistance echoes that of religious leaders in Martin Luther's time, who opposed translating the Bible from Latin to local languages. Today, on Korea's 10,000-Won bill, a portrait of King Sejong appears alongside the Hangul characters he created, symbolizing his lasting impact on Korean culture.

Uniqueness

Korea's strong cultural identity has been shaped and reinforced by its enduring and resistance to numerous foreign invasions. Global unity seems attainable in peaceful times, and a sense of world citizenship takes root. However, in times of conflict, such as the Cold War or today's U.S.-China rivalry, nations often turn inward, prioritizing their interests and fostering nationalism. When a weaker nation faces the threat of being overtaken by a foreign power, its people's drive to preserve their national identity becomes even more vital. Historian Han Young-woo discusses this in his book *A Review of Korean History*, describing how two historical texts from Korea's Goryeo period—Samguk Yusa and Jewang Ungi—reflect this sentiment. He notes,

"Both works share common themes: they begin our history with the founding of Dangun Joseon and proudly recount the legendary origins of each dynasty's founders, emphasizing a sense of identity and moral integrity. This reflects a desire to restore national pride and authenticity during the Mongol occupation."

During the early years of Japanese colonial rule in Korea, a nationalist movement emerged, led by intellectuals studying the Korean language and history to cultivate a sense of cultural pride. Various studies and publications on Hangul emerged, covering its phonetics, grammar, and structure, and newspapers written in

Hangul were published. Korea's first Institute for National Language was also founded. Independence activist Shin Chae-ho promoted patriotism by writing biographies of historical heroes like Admiral Yi Sun-shin, a revered figure in Korea today.

Attempts to explore a national identity through language studies can also be observed in other countries. A similar example is the role played by the Brothers Grimm during the early 19th century when Napoleon ruled over Germany. Neil MacGregor, in his book *Germany*, stated:

"The Grimms' fairy tales were part of a German political and social renaissance, evidence that in their language and their folk tales the Germans had an identity which no foreign invader could eradicate."

Even in modern times, Korea has maintained efforts to preserve its unique identity across various fields. With the rise of PCs, the internet, and smartphones, the world has witnessed tech giants like Google and Apple dominate. Yet Koreans have shown consistent support for homegrown products and services, resisting foreign dominance whenever possible. This trend has only strengthened as Korea's manufacturing and IT sectors have grown globally competitive. Here are some examples:

- The Korean government avoids using MS Office and opts for native software, Hangul Office. All government documents are created and distributed in this format, and any official submissions must be in Hangul Office format, leading most businesses to purchase and use it alongside MS Office. This policy reflects Korea's efforts to maintain software independence.

- Naver, not Google, is the largest search engine in Korea. Although it started as a search engine, it has become one of Korea's leading tech companies.

- KakaoTalk, developed by Kakao, is Korea's go-to messaging app. While some people use Telegram, other global messengers are barely used. Naver's LINE messenger, which did not take hold in Korea, has succeeded as the primary messaging app in Japan, Taiwan, and Thailand.

- Koreans primarily use Samsung or Apple smartphones. Samsung initially attempted to launch its mobile operating system but adopted Google's Android.

- Koreans rely on brands like LG and Samsung for laptops, TVs, refrigerators, and other large appliances. In contrast, smaller appliances from China are sometimes used but generally rate lower in quality and customer satisfaction.

- Finally, Hyundai Motor Group has a dominant market share in Korea for traditional and electric vehicles.

Resident Registration Number

In Korea, every citizen has a unique personal identification number called a Resident Registration Number (RRN) at birth. This number is used throughout a person's life, from cradle to grave, and typically does not change. (However, recent policy updates allow individuals who have suffered or are at risk of significant harm—such as identity theft or violence due to leaked information—to apply for a new RRN upon review by a government committee.) For most Koreans, a few key numbers are ingrained: RN, university student ID number, and, for men, Military service ID. The RRN is a 13-digit number with the person's birthdate in the first six digits. Koreans receive their first official ID card featuring this number at age 17.

Unlike in Western countries, where personal identification numbers (such as social security numbers) are primarily used for specific administrative purposes like social welfare or healthcare, Korea's RRN is used widely across both public and private sectors. This number is essential for administrative tasks, banking, real estate transactions, and other private activities. Although other identification numbers, like a driver's license or passport number, are sometimes used as alternative IDs, they are not nearly as commonly relied upon as the RRN.

The extensive use of a single ID number has also

led to issues. Due to multiple large-scale data breaches in the financial sector and frequent misuse of personal data, Korea's data protection laws have become increasingly strict. Therefore, almost every website now requires users to go through detailed consent procedures regarding collecting and using personal information to register.

4

Four Kingdoms over Twenty Centuries

Introduction

Korean culture, now known as Hallyu or the Korean Wave, has gained remarkable popularity across Asia and worldwide. As a result, global media is paying increasing attention to Korea, and the content that introduces Korea is rising. However, one point that stands out as a missed opportunity in some of the videos introducing Korea is that they often begin Korea's story with the Korean War. While the story of Korea's transformation from one of the world's poorest countries post-war to a booming economy is compelling and makes for a strong introduction, it seems that very few people explore the history of the Korean Peninsula before the war.

Of course, this approach is understandable, as exploring Korean history often requires confronting the complex period of Japanese colonial rule. Delving further back, especially before the 20th century, is challenging due to limited resources and, perhaps, fewer dramatic narratives.

In this chapter, I will briefly introduce the kingdoms on the Korean Peninsula before the 20th century. As an ordinary Korean with a general understanding of our history rather than a professional historian, I hope this piece will provide a lighthearted, accessible look into Korea's past.

A distinct notion of the nation

In Europe, the concept of a *nation* is often considered a relatively recent development in their long history. In the past, without modern communication like television to promote the nation's role or even roads and cars to travel to the edges of national borders, it was likely difficult for people to grasp a clear notion of a nation. Additionally, the dominant authority of the Roman Papacy likely further blurred national boundaries in the minds of Europeans. Korea's situation, however, was quite different. From the Three Kingdoms Period, beginning around the turn of the first millennium, Korea has maintained distinct and enduring kingdoms (nations) for nearly 2,000 years. While it was not until the 10th century, with the Goryeo Dynasty, that a fully centralized state emerged, we can reasonably consider the Three Kingdoms as the starting point of Korean history, where features of a nation—such as hereditary monarchy and the rule of law—were already evident. Throughout two millennia, four major dynasties each governed the Korean Peninsula for roughly 500 years on average:

- **The Three Kingdoms Period**
- **Unified Silla**
- **Goryeo**
- **Joseon**

This extended history gave the Korean people a solid and lasting image of the nation, not an imagined community. Even when viewed alongside the chronologies of other countries, the longevity of Korean dynasties is notably significant. Seoul National University professor Han Young-woo, in his book *A Review of Korean History*, provides insight into this remarkable continuity:

"It's a misconception to think that our dynasties lasted so long simply because Korean society progressed slowly. A nation, like a person, is an organic entity, and if well-governed, it can be sustained for a long time. Therefore, the longevity of a dynasty indicates effective state management. A change in dynasty is not merely a shift in power but an outcome where a reformist movement, supported by the people, arises to replace a regime that has exhausted its societal relevance."

The Three Kingdoms Period

Around the turn of the first millennium, three ancient kingdoms emerged on the Korean Peninsula:

- **Goguryeo** (Early 1st century BC – late 7th century AD)
- **Baekje** (Early 1st century BC – late 7th century AD)
- **Silla** (Early 1st century BC – early 10th century AD)

Together, these kingdoms dominated the Korean Peninsula and parts of Northeast Asia for centuries, spanning the period when the Roman Empire rose and fell in Europe. This era is known in Korean history as the Three Kingdoms Period.

Goguryeo ruled over the northern part of the peninsula (present-day North Korea) and parts of what is now northeastern China. Due to its location, Goguryeo engaged in numerous conflicts with successive Chinese dynasties, reinforcing its image as a powerful, militaristic kingdom. Goguryeo's founder, Jumong, was said to be a master archer (in fact, the name Jumong is linked to archer). In the 4th and 5th centuries, during the reigns of King Gwanggaeto The Great and his son King Jangsu, Goguryeo reached its height, expanding its territory into northeastern China and the southern part of the Korean Peninsula. Gwanggaeto, meaning expander of territory, is one of only two Korean kings honored with the title

The Great for his conquests in Korean history.

Baekje, in contrast, evokes an image of refined sophistication, often associated with elegance and artistic achievement. Located in the western part of the peninsula, including present-day Seoul, Baekje was a center of art and culture, enriched by active trade and cultural exchanges across the sea, especially with China. Baekje imported cultural influences and advanced them, particularly in metalwork. One of Baekje's finest artifacts, the Gilt-Bronze Incense Burner, is housed in the National Buyeo Museum, highlighting Baekje's excellence in metal craftsmanship. Today, Baekje's legacy can be seen in the southwestern regions of Gongju, Buyeo, and Iksan, where cultural heritage sites are well-preserved.

While Baekje lay in the west, Silla ruled the eastern region of the peninsula. Silla was known for its Hwarang, a youth group of noble lineage dedicated to cultivating both mental and physical strength, somewhat akin to today's military academies. The Hwarang played a pivotal role in unifying the three kingdoms under Silla's rule. The Hwarang spirit and their stories of loyalty and passion were featured in the 2016 KBS drama *Hwarang*, starring well-known figures such as Park Seo-joon from *Itaewon Class* and BTS's V.

Silla is also unique in Korean history for having produced three reigning queens. In Silla, only those of pure royal descent could inherit the throne; thus, if no male heir was available, a female could ascend as ruler. This distinct lineage system set Silla apart from other

Korean dynasties, often engaging in bloody struggles for the throne, underscoring Silla's strict adherence to royal lineage.

Unified Silla
(Late 7th century – early 10th century)

As the name suggests, the Unified Silla period refers to the era when Silla, one of the original Three Kingdoms, unified the Korean Peninsula until the rise of the Goryeo Dynasty. Korean historians often distinguish between the Three Kingdoms and the Unified Silla periods to emphasize the unification milestone. While the Western Roman Empire was falling, splitting into Eastern and Western Rome, and Europe was entering a chaotic era, Korea achieved its first unification, creating a stable society that allowed Buddhism and culture to flourish. However, this period of unity was short-lived, weakened by government decadence, excessive luxury, and rising rebellions from the suffering people.

Silla, including its time during the Three Kingdoms period, endured as an ancient dynasty for nearly a thousand years. Its capital, Gyeongju, is sometimes called a museum without walls due to its rich historical legacy. The entire city is a UNESCO World Heritage site, preserving Silla's cultural treasures. Notable landmarks in Gyeongju include the Seokguram Grotto, showcasing intricately detailed Buddhist art; Bulguksa Temple, known for its beautiful twin pagodas; and

Cheomseongdae, one of the oldest astronomical observatories in the world. Located southeast of Seoul, Gyeongju is only a two-hour KTX high-speed train ride from Seoul. It is highly recommended as a travel destination. In the past, Gyeongju, along with Seoraksan Mountain, was a popular field trip destination for Korean students before international travel became common.

Goryeo
(Early 10th century – late 14th century)

The Goryeo Dynasty was founded by Wang Geon, who reunified the Korean Peninsula after the fragmentation of Unified Silla. Goryeo's capital was established in Kaesong, Wang Geon's hometown, located in what is now North Korea. The name Goryeo was chosen to emphasize a connection to the ancient kingdom of Goguryeo. Wang Geon pursued a northward expansion policy and designated Pyongyang, the former Goguryeo capital and present-day capital of North Korea, as his second capital. He strengthened ties with powerful local families by marrying widely, with 29 wives and 34 children to consolidate power. During the reign of King Gwangjong, the fourth king, royal authority was solidified, and the civil service examination (gwageo) was first introduced. By the time of King Seongjong in the late 10th century, Goryeo had established a centralized bureaucracy and adopted Confucianism as its guiding state ideology, moving away from the influence of

Buddhism, which had previously played a major political role. While Goryeo experienced a period of relative stability, it later faced internal unrest and harsh rule under military dictators.

The real challenge for Goryeo, however, came from its geopolitical position. Unlike modern-day China, a unified nation of many ethnic groups, medieval China consisted of multiple states often ruled by the Han Chinese or northern ethnic groups. While the Han Chinese dynasties regarded themselves as the cultural center, they saw neighboring groups as less civilized "barbarians." Over time, powerful non-Han groups inhabited the northern territories between Goryeo and the Han Chinese states, leading to frequent territorial conflicts.

Goryeo's misfortune lay in existence at a time when northern tribes were strong while the Han Chinese states were weaker. Consequently, Goryeo faced repeated invasions by various northern tribes. The Khitans, who ruled a kingdom called Liao from the early 10th to the early 12th century, invaded Goryeo three times. The Jurchens, who founded the Jin dynasty, alternated between peace and conflict with Goryeo. However, Goryeo suffered its most devastating incursions at the hands of the Mongols, who built a vast empire. In the early 13th century, Goryeo resisted but was ultimately overwhelmed by the Mongol invasions, resulting in significant loss of life and destruction of cultural heritage, and, by the late 13th century, Goryeo fell under Mongol (Yuan) influence until the early 14th century.

During the Goryeo period, trade flourished with

nearby China, Japan, and distant Arab nations. Goryeo's sought-after exports included ginseng and high-quality paper. (Today, ginseng remains one of Korea's most popular health supplements, especially its red variant.) The modern name "Korea" originates from the term "Core" used by Arab merchants to refer to the Goryeo traders.

Joseon
(Late 14th Century – Late 19th Century)

In 1392, Yi Seong-gye overthrew the weakened Goryeo Dynasty, which had been undermined by foreign invasions, and established a new dynasty, Joseon. The capital was moved to what is now Seoul, which has served as Korea's capital for over 630 years since the founding of Joseon. Many palaces and shrines visible in Seoul today are architectural remnants from the Joseon period.

Establishing a new dynasty often requires the support of various factions with competing interests. However, once a dynasty is established, these factions tend to disrupt order by claiming rewards for their contributions. In many periods of history, early solid rulers worked to consolidate royal authority and restore hierarchy. In the Goryeo Dynasty, King Gwangjong (the 4th ruler) strengthened royal power, laying the groundwork for his son, Seongjong, to stabilize the kingdom. Similarly, in Joseon, the efforts of King Taejong (the 3rd ruler and Yi

Seong-gye's son) to strengthen royal authority enabled his son, King Sejong, to become one of Korea's most celebrated rulers.

King Sejong The Great used his stable authority to promote economic, cultural, and scientific advancements. He consistently prioritized the welfare of his people, which is evident in his most significant achievement: the creation of Hangeul, the Korean alphabet. Sejong was motivated by compassion for the ordinary people, who could not read the complex Chinese characters used by the elite at the time. Coincidentally, during the same period that the Renaissance flourished in Italy, a cultural golden age blossomed on the Korean Peninsula.

However, the Joseon ruling class disdained technology and commerce, focusing instead on Neo-Confucianism. This philosophy emphasized abstract, metaphysical concepts. Although Joseon was Yi Seong-gye's kingdom, Jeong Do-jeon, a Neo-Confucian scholar, designed its ideological foundation. Jeong envisioned Joseon as an ideal Neo-Confucian state. In the Joseon social hierarchy, the *Yangban* class (scholar-officials) occupied the top tier, dedicating their lives to studying Neo-Confucianism, while professionals such as doctors, categorized as *Jungin*, held a lower status despite their expertise.

Neo-Confucianism, also known as Zhu Xi's Confucianism, originated in China's Song Dynasty and combined Confucian ethics with metaphysical explorations. It sought to understand the principles of the universe and foster moral character. For modern audiences, neo-Confucianism may seem as esoteric as certain schools of Western philosophy.

The ruling class's inability to adapt to global changes and fixation on abstract ideals left Joseon vulnerable to external threats. At the end of the 16th century, Toyotomi Hideyoshi, who had unified Japan, invaded Joseon. The weakened Joseon military struggled to fend off the invasion, suffering significant damage. In the early 17th century, the Ming dynasty in China fell, and the Qing dynasty rose. Joseon, having previously received aid from the Ming Dynasty during the Japanese invasion, resisted the Qing, only to face a humiliating defeat by the new Chinese power.

5

True Freedom Beyond Anti-communism

The challenging journey toward democracy

Professor Park Jung-ho, now a prominent figure on YouTube, shared a memorable conversation on his channel. At a forum, he met an Indian economist who praised Korea's economic achievements but said he found something else even more astonishing—the fact that Korea's wealthiest individuals could be sent to prison. He noted that this was unthinkable in India. Korea, however, has seen even more drastic events; in 2017, then-President Park Geun-hye was impeached and imprisoned while still in office.

Korea did not obtain democracy easily. Declaring a country democratic does not mean that sovereignty naturally passes to the people. True democracy requires sustained efforts by an engaged populace demanding accountability from a powerful few. Often, this journey involves tremendous sacrifice. Korea's path to democracy was no different, marked by hardship from the start.

From the outset, Korea's journey was challenging. Korea started poorly in the late 19th century, marking the beginning of Korea's modern era. Korea endured colonial rule, and with independence came an unfamiliar ideology that ultimately led to a tragic war between people of the same nation. A brief historical summary of the beginning of modern Korea:

- **1897–1910**: The five-century-long Joseon Dynasty collapsed, establishing the Korean Empire. Korean Empire struggled with a forced opening and misread the global dynamics, eventually falling to Japanese imperialism.
- **1910–1945**: For 35 years, Korea suffered under Japan's colonial rule, enduring oppressive control.
- **1945–1950**: Japan's defeat in World War II ended Korea's colonial suffering, but instead of achieving complete independence, Korea was divided along the 38th parallel, with the Soviet Union occupying the North and the United States occupying the South.
- **1950–1953**: The Korean War began with North Korea's invasion. As the first armed conflict of the

Cold War, it was a proxy war between democratic and communist powers. For Koreans, the war was a tragic era, with compatriots forced to fight each other under ideologies they barely understood.

One might wonder if North Korea truly understood communism. Political theories usually arise as responses to specific issues in their times, requiring historical context for proper understanding. Marxism, for example, emerged in response to the Industrial Revolution and the problems within capitalism. But could North Korea, a newly liberated state fresh from colonial rule, truly grasp Marxist-Leninist communism? It seems unlikely. North Korea conducted a land reform in 1946, and soon after, its Communist Party grew from 5,000 to 270,000 members.

Did South Korea truly safeguard the liberal democracy it defended with bloodshed in the war? Not exactly. In post-war South Korea, "freedom" became synonymous with "anti-communism," meaning that the suppression of communism was equated with the protection of freedom. Under this view, military coups or extended authoritarian rule were justified as necessary to defend freedom. In the military regime, calls for genuine democracy were often branded as communist and met with harsh repression.

A key example is the May 18 Gwangju Democratic Uprising in 1980, when citizens demanded an end to martial law and the resignation of the military regime. Only to face brutal crackdowns by airborne troops, resulting in numerous casualties, the Gwangju Uprising exposed the extent of human cruelty for power, leaving a deep trauma in Korean society. The 2024 Nobel Laureate in Literature, Han Kang, drew upon this tragedy in her novel *Human Acts*.

It was not until 1987, one year before the Seoul Olympics, that Korea finally began its journey toward genuine democracy. The June Democratic Uprising, sparked by the torture and death of student activist Park Jong-cheol and the tear-gas killing of Yonsei University student Lee Han-yeol, mobilized students, workers, intellectuals, and civic groups in a broad movement. This movement ultimately won the direct presidential election reform, marking a pivotal turn in Korea's democratization process.

The President

Korea operates under a presidential system where the president is directly elected by popular vote and serves a single five-year term. Reflecting on modern Korean history, the nation's short democratic experience, challenges in establishing civilian control over the military, and a lack of robust checks on power have led to numerous turbulent events surrounding its presidents. Here are a few dramatic moments involving the presidency:

- **An 18-Year Regime Ends in Assassination**: Park Chung-hee, who came to power through a military coup in 1961 and served as Korea's president from the 5th to the 9th administrations, was assassinated in 1979 by Kim Jae-gyu, the head of the Korean CIA. While Kim cited personal grievances, including tensions with Park and frustration over being blocked from reporting to him by the head of presidential security, the full motives remain disputed.

- **Another Coup Ultimately Leads to Accountability**: Shortly after Park's assassination in 1979, another military coup was led by figures within a powerful faction in the army. (This period is dramatized in the 2023 Korean film *12.12: The Day*, which drew over 13 million viewers.) Though Koreans longed for a new democratic era, the "Seoul Spring" never came. The coup's leaders, Chun Doo-hwan and Roh Tae-woo, consecutively served as presidents from 1980 to 1993. In 1993, newly elected President Kim Young-sam dismantled the military faction's influence. Both former presidents were prosecuted and convicted of insurrection.

- **The Unchecked Dictator's Daughter Impeached**: In 2013, Park Geun-hye, the daughter of former president Park Chung-hee, became Korea's 18th president. However, allegations that unelected aides influenced national affairs led to massive candlelight protests demanding her impeachment. In 2017, she became the first Korean president to be removed from office by parliamentary impeachment while still serving.

Behind Gyeongbokgung Palace, one of Seoul's main tourist attractions and an iconic Joseon-era palace, is the Blue House, the former official residence and office of the Korean president. Once a powerful symbol of modern political history, the Blue House's era as the seat of power ended in 2022, when President Yoon Suk-yeol moved the presidential office to Yongsan and opened the Blue House to the public.

The National Assembly

Unlike countries like the United States, which has a bicameral system (Senate and House of Representatives), Korea has a single legislative body called the National Assembly. It operates independently from the executive branch, led by the president, and the judicial branch, represented by the Supreme Court. Although Korea has a multiparty system, the seats in the National Assembly have long been dominated by two major parties: the conservative People Power Party and the progressive Democratic Party. Wealthier individuals, older generations, and people from the TK region (Daegu and Gyeongsangbuk-do) lean conservative, while the middle class, younger generations, and people from Seoul and the Jeolla region tend to favor progressive policies. Given this division, Koreans avoid discussing politics with those close to them to prevent uncomfortable disagreements.

Members of the National Assembly are elected by the public, similar to the president, and serve four-year terms. Since the timing of presidential and legislative elections differ, citizens can hold the president accountable by voting against the ruling party in parliamentary elections if they are dissatisfied with national governance. Although politicians often pledge to serve the people during election campaigns, they sometimes focus more on personal power once in office, leading to a scarcity of widely respected politicians. The media, too, tends to amplify this political cynicism by emphasizing power struggles over coverage of dedicated public service, further distancing people from politics. This gap has occasionally allowed politicians to take advantage of their positions for personal gain. However, frequent power shifts between the two main parties and the scrutiny that each administration places on its predecessors' misconduct have, fortunately, led to a gradual decline in government corruption.

In addition to National Assembly representatives, Koreans directly elect local government officials, including the Mayor of Seoul, local council members, and superintendents of education (who oversee regional education systems).

6

Rich out of Poverty

Remarkable and Unique

Korea's economic growth is remarkable and unique. In the 1950s, Korea was one of the poorest countries in the world, with a bleak outlook for the future. However, today, Korea boasts the world's tenth-largest economy. The World Bank and Korea Development Institute (KDI) described this rapid growth in a joint report, noting:

"Korea sustained 29 years of rapid growth (greater than 6 percent) from 1962 to 1991 as it transitioned from a low-income to a middle-income economy, a relatively rare accomplishment (In comparison, the median duration of rapid growth in other countries was nine years)."

In addition, Korea entered the ranks of high-income economies in 1995 and joined the OECD, the organization for wealthy nations. Although its economic growth slowed briefly during the 1998 Asian Financial Crisis, Korea rebounded quickly. It rejoined the high-income economy status in 2001 and has maintained it ever since.

From the ruins of war to an emerging economy

There are complex and diverse factors behind Korea's rapid economic growth. Here, I will focus on two key aspects: how Korea transitioned from a developing country to a middle-income nation; and how it avoided the middle-income trap and advanced to a high-income economy.

Unlike many developing nations that pursued protectionist policies during early industrialization, Korea adopted an export-driven, free-trade approach to boost national competitiveness. After independence, former colonies typically faced a dilemma: whether to follow an import-substitution model to foster self-sufficiency or an export-led model to open up international trade. The former, used by nations like Argentina, Brazil, India, and Mexico, aimed to replace imported goods with domestic production to create a self-reliant economy through protective tariffs. While this model helped these countries in early industrialization, they often encountered long-term challenges due to inefficiencies in protectionism, such as decreased product quality and low competitiveness.

Instead, from the 1950s to the 1970s, Korea chose the export-led path, emphasizing labor-intensive light manufacturing industries and government-led initiatives to build these industries. Starting with the textile and garment industries, which created many jobs, Korea expanded its export-driven economy to include products like bags and shoes. The Guro Industrial Complex in Seoul, established in 1967, became a manufacturing hub, at one point responsible for 10% of Korea's total exports.

For the light industry to thrive, however, low wages alone aren't enough—product quality and productivity are essential for international competitiveness. Korea's emphasis on education proved advantageous here, as a generally educated workforce contributed to higher productivity in light manufacturing. After the Korean War, education was seen as a path out of poverty, and even amid the Korean War, schools remained operational, with a portion of U.S. aid allocated to building schools. By the late 1950s, elementary school enrollment rates reached 96%.

While Korea's industrialization was government-led, the backbone of this effort was young female laborers. Though today, low birth rates are a concern in Korea, large families in the 1950s and 1960s were typical, often leading families to concentrate resources on the eldest son, with daughters sacrificing to support the family. Many young women joined the workforce instead of pursuing higher education, working in factories by day, and attending night schools to continue their studies.

Avoiding the middle-income trap

Many developing countries achieve rapid growth to reach middle-income status, only to stall due to slowing productivity and never advance to high-income economies—a phenomenon known as the "middle-income trap." How did Korea manage to escape this trap and become an advanced economy?

In Korea, there is a saying called *jeon-ae-wi-bok*, which means that a situation where something terrible happens turns out to be positive through effort and determination to overcome it. Korea progressed through phases of industrialization: light industry in the 1960s, heavy industries like steel, machinery, and shipbuilding in the 1970s, and then tech-centered industries such as electronics and automotive in the 1980s. This trajectory positioned Korea as a newly advanced economy by the 1990s, even marked by its entry into the OECD in 1995. However, the 1997 Asian Financial Crisis (the "IMF crisis" in Korea) delivered a significant economic blow. The IMF required Korea to adopt various neoliberal economic policies in exchange for bailout loans. The government implemented deep structural reforms: labor market flexibility through corporate restructuring, improved corporate transparency, debt reduction, privatization of public enterprises, deregulation, and financial market liberalization. Although these changes caused social issues like widespread unemployment and income inequality, they ultimately strengthened Korea's economic resilience and corporate foundations, laying the groundwork for the country's transition from a middle-income to a high-income economy. Remarkably, Korea repaid its IMF loans in full within just four years.

The emergence of the internet in the 1990s also came at a fortuitous time. As we all experienced, the rise of the internet transformed lives and businesses globally. In the late 1990s, Korea invested heavily in broadband infrastructure, betting on the information age to reinvigorate its economy amid the IMF crisis. This led to a focused effort to foster IT-related ventures, which enabled small and medium-sized enterprises (SMEs) to gain a foothold in an economy previously dominated by large conglomerates. As SMEs grew, employment surged, driving a diversification from a manufacturing-heavy economy to one with a significant service sector.

Ultimately, Korea seized the opportunities of the IMF crisis and the information age, using them as springboards to leap over the middle-income trap and join the ranks of advanced economies.

The shadows of economic growth

At some point, Korea became wealthy, at least by economic indicators. However, a few favorable numbers do not capture everyone's quality of life. One of Korea's most pressing issues is the growing economic inequality. Although Seoul constantly expands with new buildings, most of these properties are owned by a few wealthy individuals, and this concentration of wealth is only intensifying. This trend often stems from benefits that these individuals' families received in the past. When Korea struggled economically, the government invested its limited capital in select corporations, creating a system where only a handful of companies reaped the rewards. This is similar to a family that invests all its resources in sending the eldest son to college while other siblings sacrifice, only for that eldest son to believe his success was entirely self-made.

Consequently, the voices of those who sacrificed—many of them everyday citizens—have long called for a more equitable sharing of the fruits of economic growth. Yet, when progressive governments try to address this by focusing more on public welfare, certain conservative media and groups react strongly. They use struggling welfare states as examples, warning that Korea will face similar economic ruin if it prioritizes social welfare. This stance is akin to someone who has never gained weight obsessing over the risk of obesity.

In Korea, support and empathy for society's most vulnerable are in short supply. In a country where rapid economic growth is almost universally seen as a virtue, welfare is often dismissed as a vice. Korea has devoted itself almost exclusively to growth, concentrating all capital toward this goal, bringing considerable economic success. However, as a tool for redistributing resources, welfare has been cast as threatening to weaken growth. Some figures reveal society's hidden struggles. Korea has the highest suicide rate and elderly poverty rate among OECD nations. Yet, the country has been unable to fully support the needs of its vulnerable citizens, partly due to negative perceptions of welfare. A troubling reality is that this competitive society tends to blame those who fall behind, viewing even minimal support for them as unfair.

Real estate

Koreans place a high value on how others perceive them, which often drives a desire for social recognition. Many seek to establish status by displaying wealth, with cars and houses as critical symbols. While people generally consider comfort when choosing a car, there is a popular twist on this idea in Korea. Instead of "ride comfort" (Seung-cha-gam in Korean), people talk about "exit impression" (Ha-cha-gam in Korean). This term reflects the attention (and envy) one gets when stepping out of a nice car, with the assumption that pricier cars create a more significant impression.

If cars indicate someone's financial comfort, a person's home is a substantial measure of wealth. In Korea, real estate is the preferred form of investment, with roughly 80% of household assets tied up in property. Knowing where someone lives can provide a general sense of their financial standing because home ownership is a significant indicator of wealth.

Koreans' love for real estate also stems from the belief that property values only go up. Although this isn't always true, the general trend has met expectations, with property prices increasing significantly, especially during COVID-19, when low interest rates flooded the market with liquidity. Another unique factor driving property prices up is Korea's distinctive rental system, known as *jeonse*. This option lies between owning and renting; it allows people to pay a large deposit, often 50-70% of a home's value, to live there for two years without monthly rent. Jeonse enables people with less capital to own property with the tenant's deposit covering a large portion of the purchase price—a strategy known as *gap investment*, a form of leveraged investment. If property prices rise, this leverage allows for a significant profit with relatively little initial capital.

Excessive increases in real estate prices are a source of frustration for young adults, who are often priced out of the market. High property prices make it difficult for young people to start independent lives and save for the future. For instance, the housing market spike during the COVID-19 era left many young, first-time buyers disheartened. With limited savings, some have turned to riskier investments like cryptocurrency, hoping for quicker returns.

7

Believer Below 40%

Introduction

The history of Western and Middle Eastern cultures is inseparable from religion. In Korea, however, this is different. Suppose a foreigner asks me what the primary religion of my country is. In that case, I find it difficult to answer right away. Buddhism entered Korea long ago but was politically marginalized from the 14th century onwards. Confucianism, often considered an East Asian religion, has some religious aspects but is closer to a governing philosophy and social norms than a traditional faith. Christianity, which arrived in Korea later, now has the most adherents but does not represent the nation.

Currently, a significant portion of Koreans identify as non-religious, and the trend of secularization is growing stronger. According to a 2021 Gallup Korea survey, 40%

of Koreans have a religion, with Protestantism at 17%, Catholicism at 6%, and Buddhism at 16%. Although many Koreans are non-religious, it is not accurate to label them all as strictly materialistic. Many are interested in spiritual matters and may seek religious or spiritual engagement, even if they do not formally belong to any faith.

A 2023 study from the Korean Pastoral Data Institute also showed that the number of religious people is decreasing (with 37% identifying as religious and 63% as non-religious). This trend has led to a decline in new clergy and Buddhist monks. Professor Lee Jung-chul, who spoke at the 2024 Sociology of Religion Conference in Korea, offered this perspective on secularization in Korea:

"As a Christian, it's common also to visit Buddhist temples or have experiences with shamanism; there is very little apprehension about crossing these boundaries. Additionally, rather than fully committing to one faith, people often choose various religious practices based on personal needs."

In Korea, there is relatively little conflict between religions, and different faiths coexist peacefully. Buddha's birthday and Christmas are national holidays, and prominent politicians commonly attend both ceremonies regardless of their personal beliefs. In general, Koreans view other religions with tolerance. Once, I picked up a free church newsletter on the street, and it shared an interesting story: kiwi birds in New Zealand, having no natural predators for many years, eventually lost the need to fly. But when people arrived, the kiwis became nocturnal to avoid humans. The article used this story to caution against complacency, likening people to kiwis and suggesting that without growth, we risk decline. I was somewhat surprised by the church's flexible use of evolutionary theory as an example.

Religion in Korea seems flexible and somewhat relaxed. Seeing the ongoing conflict between Israel and nearby Islamic countries reinforces this feeling. I can intellectually grasp the Crusades and other religious wars around the world, but emotionally, it is hard to relate. This is true not only for me but for most Koreans. In Korean society, religious fanaticism is generally seen as unfavorable. People whose daily lives are dominated by their religious beliefs are often found in pseudo-religion rather than mainstream religions.

Additionally, Koreans do not necessarily follow their parents' faith traditions; this is particularly common in Catholicism and Buddhism. Many who attended services with their parents as children stopped going to church or temple once they reached adulthood. In a lighthearted way, someone might even mention their childhood baptism to emphasize their high morals jokingly.

Protestant Christianity, however, is relatively community-orientated, with churches forming large communities. It is common to see friends continuing to attend the church they attended as children.

People here are also open-minded about conversions. For example, if we hear that an ordinary friend suddenly became a monk, we would be curious to know why.

However, if a friend we once knew as a Buddhist now attends a church, we would usually think that could be possible.

Buddhism

Buddhism is the oldest religion in Korea, and it was introduced in China around the 4th century during the Three Kingdoms period. A visit to a museum quickly reveals how Buddhism captivated people's hearts. At the National Museum of Korea in Yongsan, Seoul, you can see the Gilt-bronze Pensive Maitreya Bodhisattva statue, which is believed to date back to this period. Observing the serene smile on this statue offers a glimpse into the compassion at the core of Buddhism. Buddhism flourished even more during the Goryeo Dynasty, reaching the status of a state religion. However, with the founding of the Joseon Dynasty, which prioritized Confucianism, Buddhism's influence waned. Buddhist temples were moved from city centers to remote mountains, and Buddhism became primarily associated with women. Had Joseon continued Goryeo's embrace of Buddhism, Korea might have grand religious structures in city centers, much like the cathedrals in European cities.

Instead, Buddhism found a unique role, offering solace to people in remote, secluded spaces. During past authoritarian regimes, democracy activists took refuge in mountain temples to escape government oppression.

Law exam candidates, seeking freedom from worldly distractions, sometimes prepared for their exams in temples. Once they returned to their everyday lives, these secluded spaces became famous for people seeking inner peace through meditation. Temple Stay programs, which allow visitors to stay at temples and experience Buddhist traditions and meditation practices, have remained popular for many years. Launched initially to accommodate the shortage of lodging and introduce Korean culture to foreigners during the 2002 World Cup, the program is now over 20 years old. In 2017, a record four million people participated, which has likely grown. Temple Stay is more of a short-term meditation retreat than a religious experience.

Catholicism

Catholicism was introduced to Korea in the late 16th and early 17th centuries as a part of Seohak, or "Western Learning," which initially combined Western academic ideas with religious teachings. Remarkably, Korea is one of the few countries where Catholicism spread without priests. In the early days, Korean Catholics chose bishops and priests among themselves to practice their faith, unaware that lay-led worship wasn't allowed under church law. Upon learning this, they quickly requested priests from abroad.

Establishing Catholicism in the Joseon Dynasty was challenging, as it clashed with the deeply rooted

Confucian culture and got caught up in political conflicts, leading to severe persecution and many martyrs.

In Korea, statues of the Virgin Mary are commonly placed at the entrance of churches. Even the names of Catholic hospitals are ST. Mary's Hospital. As a child, I used to wonder if Catholics worshipped Mary instead of Jesus because of the statues. Regarding this tradition, Father Song Young-oh from the Diocese of Suwon explained in an article for Gyeonggi Ilbo:

"When Korean churches were established, they began placing statues of the Virgin Mary at the entrance, rather than statues of the church's patron saint, as is often done abroad. Historically, this may relate to the dedication of the Korean Church to the Virgin Mary by Korea's first priest, Saint Andrew Kim Dae-geon. Yet, it also reflects Koreans' profound respect for maternal love, which parallels their view of God's love. This desire for Mary's protection has fostered a special devotion to her among Korean Catholics."

Catholicism also played a significant role in advancing democracy in Korea. During the military regime, even casual remarks could land someone in prison. Catholic churches courageously advocated for democracy through their masses and became sanctuaries for democracy activists during intense protests. Police were often reluctant to enter churches to apprehend protesters who had sought refuge there.

Protestantism

Protestantism was the last of Korea's three major religions, introduced in the late 19th century by British and American missionaries. Although Protestantism initially spread more smoothly than Catholicism, it faced significant oppression during the Japanese occupation of Korea. Protestant missionaries established private schools, introducing modern ideas and instilling Koreans with independence and patriotism, inspiring many independence activists.

After the Korean War, Protestantism expanded rapidly alongside Korea's economic growth. In the 1960s, as government-led development policies led to mass migration from rural areas to cities, Protestant churches provided newcomers with a place of spiritual refuge and support, often growing into megachurches. For example, Yoido Full Gospel Church, one of the largest megachurches in the world, had nearly one million members as of 2020.

Korea has many large churches and countless small neighborhood churches or church plants. If we compare religions to businesses, Catholicism and Buddhism in Korea are like a franchise with a central headquarters managing many official branches, similar to Starbucks. Protestantism, however, is closer to a network of independent businesses. Just as small businesses must work even harder to compete with large franchises, these small Protestant churches are often extra dedicated to sustaining their presence. This may explain why red crosses from many small churches are a prominent part of Korea's nighttime cityscapes.

Self-made individuals often share a common trait: they rarely listen to others. Imagine a pastor who built a small, struggling church into a large, thriving congregation. How might they feel as they approach retirement and their grown child enters the same profession? Despite ongoing efforts within churches to address this issue, the privatization and inheritance of megachurches remain persistent problems. I wonder if they might blame external factors for the decline in religious followers these days instead of looking inward.

Shamanism

Shamanism has been deeply intertwined with Korean life for centuries. One of its most iconic rituals is the gut, a ceremony featuring lively music, dynamic dancing, and a connection to the spiritual realm to heal the client's pain and sorrow. The gut has also influenced traditional Korean music, such as Pansori and folk songs. Beyond solving personal problems, the gut was performed for the well-being of entire communities. A famous example is the Gangneung Danoje Festival, recognized as a UNESCO Intangible Cultural Heritage.

As Korea became more urbanized, the noisy gut ceremonies largely disappeared, and shamans moved into cities to quietly offer spiritual reading instead. Koreans are deeply interested in divination, often visiting shamans to seek answers to life's challenges or guidance about an uncertain future. As I mentioned earlier, religion in Korea tends to be somewhat flexible, and even Christians frequently consult shamans. Common questions include whether they should marry their current partner, if changing jobs is the right move, what to avoid, whether their business will succeed, and when they might achieve wealth and success. Today's shamans have adapted to modern times, with many becoming active on platforms like YouTube.

Shamanism's popularity is also reflected in Korean cinema. For example, the highest-grossing Korean film in 2024 was *Exhuma* (Pamyoh), an occult mystery about strange events that unfold when a geomancer, an undertaker, and shamans relocate a suspicious grave. With around 12 million viewers, the film became the year's biggest box-office hit. (In Korea, surpassing 10 million viewers is considered the benchmark for a blockbuster.)

Who Becomes a Shaman? It is rare for someone to become a shaman simply because their parents were. But family influence can play a role. It is known that many who became shamans have relatives who were also shamans. Most shamans begin as ordinary members of society but experience sudden, unexplained illnesses before receiving a spiritual calling, known as a Sin-naerim, to become a shaman. Interestingly, frequent clients of shamans believe their spiritual abilities have an expiration date and prefer newly initiated shamans who have recently undergone the Sin-naerim.

Even outside the context of professional shamans, shamanistic beliefs remain ingrained in Korean culture. For example, Taemong, or "conception dreams," are widely accepted and deeply meaningful. These vivid dreams are usually experienced by close family members, such as the husband or parents, early in pregnancy. Unlike ordinary dreams, Taemong is remarkably distinct—common examples include holding a large fish or eating an enormous peach.

8
One-Size-Fits-None Education

School education

In Korea, children start elementary school the year after they turn six. They attend school for a total of 12 years before entering university. Elementary school lasts six years, which is quite long compared to the three years each spent in middle and high school, which fly by.

Children are born with diverse talents, but schools often fail to nurture them all. Instead, they focus almost exclusively on academic skills, becoming places where students are evaluated and ranked through tests. As a result, students are forced to dedicate most of their time and energy to studying and exams. This approach is like a clothing store offering only one style and size, regardless of each customer's unique body type or fashion preference. Customers have no choice but to squeeze themselves into the pre-made outfit. Although times have changed since I was a student, schools remain the same. They still impose standardized knowledge on students and use exams to rank them. While exams are intended to assess students' understanding of what they have learned, schools are more focused on determining who ranks where. Sometimes, exams even include questions beyond what schools have taught.

For these reasons, as I will discuss later, many students attend private academies (Hagwon in Korean) after school to keep up.

Korean society has evolved and developed significantly, so why do schools only offer a "one-size-fits-all" education? There are two main reasons.

First, schools are caught between past successes and the need to adapt to a changing world. In Korea's earlier days, particularly during industrialization, the country needed a highly skilled workforce to support its growing manufacturing industries. Schools played a critical role by producing workers with standardized knowledge and strong academic skills. This "factory-like" education system contributed to Korea's economic success by quickly supplying industries with competent labor. While this approach was practical in the past, times have changed. Many factories have since moved to countries like China for cheaper labor. Despite this shift, schools continue to produce "factory-model" workers. Although educators know this problem, they have yet to find a solution.

Second, and perhaps more importantly, Korea emphasizes academic credentials overwhelmingly. People highly value diplomas from prestigious universities such as Seoul National University, Korea University, and Yonsei University, believing these degrees are essential to upward social mobility. This societal obsession with academic pedigree leaves schools unable to ignore the pressures of university entrance exams.

This fixation on academic hierarchy has deep historical roots. Korea's version of the civil service exam, the Gwageo, was introduced in the late 10th century during the Goryeo Dynasty. The Gwageo, which determined government positions based on individual merit rather than family background, became one of the few ways for people to rise in social status. It remained a cornerstone of Korean society for nearly 1,000 years until the country's modernization, and its legacy lives on today in the form of competitive university entrance exams. This historical precedence has pushed schools to focus almost entirely on preparing students for these exams, reducing education to a mere pathway to college admissions.

The intense world of private education

Most parents in Korea want their children to get into a prestigious university—or, these days, even more so, to enter a lucrative medical school. Although school education has become focused on college admissions, many parents feel it is insufficient, which has fueled a relentless private education craze.

Children typically attend private academies even before they start elementary school. After regular school hours, they almost always head straight to these academies, often attending on weekends. The main subjects taught at private academies are Korean, English, and math. By high school, students add more subjects like science to their schedules. These are the same subjects taught in school, yet they are retaught at private academies, wasting time and resources significantly.

Private academies focus on helping students prepare for university entrance exams and improve their school records. Many also exploit parents' anxieties by encouraging "preemptive learning," where children study material years ahead of their grade level. For example, a first-grader might study second or third-grade content. Private academies often pressure parents by warning them that their children will fall behind peers already engaging in preemptive learning. This fear-based marketing drives profits for private academies.

It is common to find private academies specializing in just one subject around schools or residential areas. Large private academy chains operate like franchise businesses, much like fast-food restaurants. In Seoul, neighborhoods like Daechi-dong and Mok-dong are famous for their dense clusters of private academies. It is easy to spot buildings filled with dozens of academies in these areas. Some star private academy instructors earn more than medical doctors, highlighting how lucrative this industry has become.

Social issues

The overheated competition for college admissions and the resulting private education craze has caused various social problems. First and foremost, private education is highly costly and places a significant financial burden on households. According to Statistics Korea, the average monthly private education expense for a high school student in Seoul in 2023 was approximately 1 million won (about $750). This figure represents an average, and the median is likely even higher. Another survey by Maeil Business Newspaper revealed that private education expenses account for an average of 21% of household spending, and around 80% of families report feeling financially strained by these costs.

Despite the growing burden, cutting back on private education spending is difficult. Most parents view it as an investment to increase their child's chances of getting into a good university. In Korea, very few parents skimp on their child's education. Every parent invests as much as they can afford. The problem is that excessive spending on private education often jeopardizes parents' retirement plans. The peak earning years for most workers are in their 50s, which coincides with the period when education expenses are at their highest. Consequently, many parents struggle to save adequately for their future.

I believe the private education craze will not go away anytime soon. Even though the job market has become increasingly competitive—making it difficult to secure good positions even with a degree from a prestigious university—parents' lofty ambitions for their children remain as strong as ever.

There is a more critical issue behind this: the burden of private education costs contributes to Korea's low birth rate. Families hesitate to have multiple children because the associated education costs can be overwhelming. One of the biggest concerns for parents considering having more children is whether their income can cover all the educational expenses.

The greatest victims of this private education craze are the students themselves. A student who is genuinely interested in studying will do so, even without pressure from parents. But how many students are genuinely motivated on their own? Many are forced into private academies by their parents, leaving them to endure immense academic stress.

This stress has led to tragic outcomes. According to Statistics Korea, the teenage suicide rate in 2023 reached a record high of 7.9 per 100,000 people. Whenever I see such statistics, I cannot help but question whether we truly live in a "better" world. Every time I realize I am becoming complicit in this system without making any effort to change it, I can't help but feel bitter.

9
Beyond The Uniform

Military service

What is the most terrifying nightmare for Korean men? It is not ghosts—it is dreaming about being back in the military. Imagine knowing, even vaguely, that you have already completed your service yet again, finding yourself in uniform. That is genuinely a spine-chilling dream.

The popular drama *My Mister* features a line that goes like this:

"All the rigid humans are what a pity. It tells me the days they have lived. Children who are hurt become adults too early."

This line is spoken by the main character, played by Lee Sun-kyun, as he sympathizes with the protagonist, played by IU, who lives her life with a perpetually rigid expression. In Korea, military service is not a choice. The military plays a significant role in shaping the lives of all Korean men. For many, it is a process that turns young boys into rigid-faced adults.

All Korean men born in Korea are required to enlist once they reach adulthood. When I served, the mandatory service period was 26 months. It has since been reduced to 18 months. Young boys often feel an overwhelming fear when they first learn that they must eventually serve. However, as they grow up and see older brothers returning from the military and friends courageously enlisting, they gradually accept their fate.

Most Korean men enlist in their early 20s, often taking a break from college. This timing makes sense, as it is when they are at their physical peak. But there is another practical reason: while conscription can be deferred until after college, finding a job post-military is much harder for graduates. Employers typically prefer fresh graduates, not those who have just returned from military service.

Have you ever held or fired a gun? Most ordinary people have not. Guns are typically restricted to soldiers, police officers, and a few others. Of course, the U.S.—where guns are much easier to obtain—is an exception. Still, I doubt every American has handled or fired a gun.

Serving in the military means learning to handle and shoot a gun as part of basic training. Some individuals, due to religious beliefs, refuse to carry firearms. For most, though, the first time holding and firing a real gun is a surreal experience. It feels like stepping into the role of a movie hero, wielding something small yet deceptively powerful.

Now that many years have passed since my discharge, I have not had any reason to hold a gun again—and hopefully never will. But if war broke out and I had to pick up a gun again, I wonder: would I survive, like a protagonist in an action film?

Military service has its advantages. The military's hierarchical structure serves as a unique training ground for leadership. Upon enlisting, recruits start at the lowest rank and focus solely on completing assigned tasks. However, as time passes and they rise through the ranks, they are inevitably required to step forward and lead their unit. This involves making critical decisions and taking full responsibility for the outcomes. Through these experiences, men grow into adults who understand and embrace responsibility.

The impact of military service seems to extend beyond the individual to influence society as a whole. Even in societies with a strong sense of civic responsibility, individuals often prioritize personal interests over collective well-being during times of significant crisis—a human tendency. However, conscription represents a sacrifice of personal interests for the greater collective need for national security. Military life provides a firsthand experience of patriotism, which proves invaluable in moments of national crisis, fostering unity over division.

For instance, during the 1997 Asia Financial Crisis, Korea faced the brink of national bankruptcy as many companies collapsed. In response, citizens voluntarily launched a gold collection campaign to bolster the country's gold reserves and improve its credit rating. People sold personal items like wedding rings and baby gifts for this cause. While the campaign alone did not single-handedly resolve the crisis, it was a remarkable display of collective determination, demonstrating that unified efforts can overcome any challenge. Korea not only weathered the crisis but emerged more robust and more resilient.

The COVID-19 pandemic offers another example. Faced with an unprecedented global health crisis, Koreans trusted the government's public health measures and adhered to them diligently. Many made conscious efforts to minimize actions that could harm others, and this collective discipline became a cornerstone in the nation's swift and effective pandemic response.

In the military, you may occasionally encounter a villain. Military service brings together people from all walks of life—those from Seoul and rural areas, cities and countryside, older and younger people, students, and working professionals. They are similar but sometimes very different. The issue with mandatory conscription is that even troublemakers, or villains, inevitably end up in the military. In the strict hierarchical structure of the military, junior soldiers under the command of a villainous senior often feel as helpless as mice facing a cat.

Unlike civilian life, the military offers no escape; you can't transfer elsewhere because you dislike the environment. Prolonged harassment from such individuals has, at times, led to tragic incidents within the military, including firearm-related accidents. Netflix's D.P. focuses on desertion, but desertion is relatively rare in military life.

Military service gives you a robust and healthy body but often feels like it clears your mind of all prior knowledge. Many soldiers joke about how "their brains have hardened." Skills like cleaning a rifle or digging with a shovel become second nature, but calculus and academic concepts feel like distant memories. Returning to college as an empty-head veteran is a tough adjustment. They face brilliant younger students who seem way ahead, looming graduation, a stack of F grades from pre-enlistment days, and rapidly changing fashion trends. Yet, those who survive, even the villains in the military, often navigate college life successfully and eventually make their way into the real world.

North Korea

South Korea is often misunderstood as a dangerous place because of North Korea. North Korea frequently launches missiles, and every time it happens, it makes headlines around the world. Given these missile tests, people unfamiliar with the situation often ask if it's safe to live in South Korea. Contrary to their concerns, life in South Korea goes as usual without alarm or panic. Most

South Koreans do not believe these missiles will land on their soil. They view North Korea's missile launches as displays of power aimed at showing off to the West.

More importantly, South Koreans are not afraid of North Korea's missiles due to the significant military gap between the two countries. North Korea relies on outdated, conventional weapons, while South Korea is equipped with state-of-the-art technology and is among the world's leading arms exporters. South Korea also allocates about 10% of its national budget to defense spending every year, an enormous figure, especially given the economic disparity between the two Koreas.

South Korea and North Korea have grown increasingly distant. The Korean War broke out in 1950, and as of 2024, the Korean Peninsula has been divided for 80 years. Even within families, long-term estrangement can turn people into strangers. Between nations, the effect is magnified. Imagine if North Korea had evolved into a typical communist state like China or Russia during this time—relations with South Korea would likely be better than they are now. Instead, North Korea became a closed-off, dynastic regime unlike anything else in the world.

Since the end of the Cold War, the relationship between the two Koreas has primarily depended on which political party is in power in South Korea. When progressive administrations are in charge, relations tend to be more peaceful, but tensions and confrontations often escalate under conservative governments. Regardless of politics, South Korean society has shifted to prioritize individual interests over collective ideals. As a result, North Korea feels increasingly like a distant "other" to most South Koreans.

Attitudes toward reunification have also evolved. A well-known Korean children's song *Our Wish* expresses a long-standing hope for reunification:

> Our wish is unification,
> Even in our dreams, unification,
> With all our hearts, unification,
> Let's make unification happen.
> Unification that saves this nation,
> Unification that saves our people,
> Unification comes quickly,
> Unification, we are waiting.

This song embodies the longing for reunification and has been sung for decades in both South and North Korea. But is it still as popular in South Korea today? Not really. Public sentiment around reunification has shifted significantly. According to a 2024 survey conducted by Seoul National University's Institute for Peace and Unification Studies, negative opinions about reunification are now almost equal to positive ones. Among younger generations, opposition to reunification even outweighs support.

The long division of the peninsula and the growing frustration with North Korea have led many South Koreans to question whether reunification is still their wish. Few people today argue that reunification is necessary simply because North and South Koreans are the same ethnic group. Instead, they weigh the potential costs and benefits, with many worrying about the economic burden and social disruptions that reunification might bring.

__10__

Go-To Getaway

Jeju Island

Jeju Island is one of the most beloved travel destinations for Koreans. It is the largest island in Korea, located off the southwestern tip of the Korean Peninsula. Jeju is just an hour's flight from Seoul, and as Korea's top tourist spot, it boasts the highest number of daily flights between the two cities. At the rooftop observation deck of Jeju Airport, you can watch planes take off and land every five minutes.

What makes Jeju unique is its volcanic landscape, which is rare in Korea. At the center of the island lies Hallasan, a towering volcano with a crater lake called Baengnokdam at its summit. Scattered across the island are numerous smaller volcanic craters, known locally as Oreum, and underground lava tubes formed by ancient lava flows. As a result, visiting Jeju feels like stepping into a foreign land, even though it's so close to Seoul. Songs celebrating Jeju's charm often evoke images of its pristine blue sea, black volcanic rocks along the coast, neatly stacked stone walls, and the endless tangerine orchards beyond those walls.

One of Jeju's highlights is the Olle Trail, a famous series of walking paths. It consists of 27 routes stretching a total of 437 kilometers. These trails meander along the coastline, connecting alleys, mountain paths, fields, beaches, and craters, with some even circling small islands off Jeju's coast. The Olle Trail introduced Koreans, who previously focused mainly on hiking, to walking tours. Following its success, countless trails have since been developed on the mainland. In spring 2019, I explored routes 5 and 6 along Jeju's southern coast. The scenery was so breathtaking that walking alone never felt lonely.

Jeju's signature dish is samgyeopsal (pork belly). On your first evening in Jeju, it's a must-try. While pork belly is available everywhere in Korea, Jeju's version is unique. The pigs raised on the island are of a different breed, making the fatty layers of the meat particularly tender and flavorful. Grilled to perfection and dipped in Jeju-style meljeot (a fermented anchovy sauce), it's delicious. Other famous dishes include galchi-jorim (braised cutlassfish) and jeonbok-juk (abalone porridge).

Jeju's high appeal as a travel destination once sparked a wave of people moving there to embrace the Jeju lifestyle. However, it took a little while for many to realize that living there differs from vacationing. Those who relocated to Jeju were often disappointed by the lack of stable jobs, high cost of living, expensive housing, and limited medical facilities. Many eventually returned to their original homes.

East coast

Unlike Jeju Island, which requires a flight, Korea's east coast is a getaway you can reach anytime by car. It offers cream-colored sandy beaches with clear blue waters, and if you turn around, towering green mountains greet you. And it's pretty close to Seoul. The most popular tourist cities along the east coast are Gangneung, Sokcho, and Yangyang.

Gangneung is famous for its coffee. While Gyeongpodae—a scenic spot where a lake meets the sea—remains a must-visit, tourists are now more drawn to the trendy coffee shops nestled among the coastal pine forests. Why is Gangneung, far removed from the global coffee belt, renowned for coffee? It started with Korea's first-generation baristas settling there and opening cafés, which grew in popularity, drawing numerous others to follow suit. Today, Anmok Beach is lined almost entirely with cafés, creating a surreal coastal coffee culture. Many of these successful Gangneung cafés have even opened branches in Seoul. In 2018, when the Winter Olympics were held in nearby Pyeongchang, transportation infrastructure improved significantly, including the establishment of a KTX (Korea's high-speed rail) station in Gangneung. This made Gangneung an even more popular destination for day trips from Seoul.

Gangneung holds a special place in my heart. When asked where I'm from, I always say Gangneung. I grew up in a rural village near the city. My playground was the mountains, fields, and streams; I always felt like I had everything. But occasional trips to the city made me acutely aware of what I didn't have. I felt embarrassed by the dirt on my shoes and envied the paved lives of city dwellers. When I entered college in Seoul, I left Gangneung behind. I dreamed of the city's allure on the night bus to Seoul, listening to Scorpions' *Big City Nights*. Yet, over time, I realized what nature had given me: a heart imprinted with blue skies and warm sunshine. It's a feeling of fulfillment beyond words.

Sokcho, an hour's drive north of Gangneung, is home to Seoraksan, considered Korea's most beautiful mountain. Famous for its vibrant autumn foliage, Seoraksan attracts countless hikers every fall. Sokcho is a harmonious blend of mountains, sea, and food. The city's culinary culture has also been shaped by its proximity to North Korea. After the Korean War, many people who could not return to their northern homes settled in Sokcho, bringing unique food traditions that now enrich the city's flavors.

Yangyang dreams of becoming Korea's Ibiza. Once overlooked between the well-known destinations of Gangneung and Sokcho, Yangyang has emerged as a hotspot for young travelers—thanks to surfing. At some point, more people began hitting the waves along Yangyang's beaches, and young crowds soon followed. Surf by day, party at night: Yangyang has quickly transformed into a haven for Korea's younger generation seeking freedom and fun.

Busan

Busan is Korea's second-largest city and the farthest major city from Seoul. It takes about 2.5 hours to reach Busan by high-speed train from Seoul. Unlike the smaller east coast cities mentioned earlier, where the sea is typically a short drive from town, Busan feels like Seoul by the sea. Busan boasts more skyscrapers than Seoul. Its beachfront skyline with towering buildings evokes vibes reminiscent of Hong Kong or New York. Busan's most famous beaches are Haeundae Beach and Gwangalli Beach.

One of the highlights of any trip is food; Busan is no exception. Close to Busan Station, you'll find three significant markets clustered together. Jagalchi Market, one of Korea's oldest seafood markets, offers a fascinating glimpse into the country's rich marine delicacies. The array of street foods at the traditional Gukje Market and Bupyeong Kkangtong Market will delight your taste buds and eyes alike. A tip for visitors: don't overeat at one stall. Think of the markets like a buffet and sample a little from several vendors. Otherwise, you might fill up too quickly and miss out on trying other dishes.

When I think of Busan, noir films come to mind. Busan, a dark and shadowy port city, provides a perfect backdrop for stories of crime and violence. The fishy scent of the harbor, its seemingly looser border controls compared to an airport, secretive shipping containers, harsh local dialects, and the rhythmic chopping of fish knives—all of these elements could serve as classic noir tropes. Dominating Korea's image of port cities, Busan has been the setting for countless Korean films. Fittingly, this cinematic city hosts the Busan International Film Festival (BIFF). This annual autumn celebration attracts filmmakers and movie lovers worldwide.

Pension (Korean-Style Vacation Home)

In Korea, a long-standing equivalent to Airbnb is called pensions. These rental cottages are the perfect escape for those seeking to recharge in nature, surrounded by mountains, forests, and water. Most pensions are located in rural areas or nestled deep in the mountains. While country folk visiting the city might stay in hotels or motels, city dwellers heading to the countryside almost always choose a pension.

Evening plans at a pension nearly always involve an outdoor barbecue—it's practically a national ritual in Korea. Just as stepping into the airport's departure gate is the most exciting moment of an overseas trip, the genuine excitement of a pension getaway begins when you leave the local Hanaro Mart with bags brimming with meat and alcohol. (Hanaro Mart is a popular franchise supermarket in rural Korea.)

The key to a good barbecue lies in the fire. Managing charcoal at a pension often becomes an unexpected challenge for first-timers. This leads to a newfound appreciation for Korean barbecue restaurants' expertly prepared charcoal grills. But there's no need to worry. Most pension owners are happy to step in as your personal Prometheus, handing over a perfectly prepared fire for an additional fee.

About The Author

He was born in Gangneung, Korea, graduated from Korea University with a degree in Industrial Engineering, and worked in asset management for over twenty years. He is also an amateur painter and the author of *Korean Word Power*.

He sees himself as a country mouse, nostalgic for the nature he left behind as a child, and a city mouse, comfortably settled in urban convenience. He takes pride in helping foreigners learn Korean through YouTube and books but sometimes feels discouraged when heartfelt thanks replace financial rewards. While he often feels sad about not translating every burst of inspiration onto a canvas, he knows how to compromise and bring his artwork to completion. Living in an era where memories fade, he strives to leave something behind—through paintings or writing—while investing in companies that store digital memories.

Notes

On The Street

Lee Min-woo, *The 'Convenience Store Kingdom' Korea Surpasses Japan in Per Capita Store Count*, Digital Times, July 20, 2024
KCCI Market Research Team, *2023 Domestic Business Closure Rate Analysis and Countermeasures Report*, 2024
Michael Pollan, *The Omnivore's Dilemma*, DDWorld Publishing, 2007
Mark Fairlie, *The 10 Largest E-Commerce Markets in the World by Country*, business.com, May 14, 2024
Lee Seung-woo, *Telecom Companies' Direct Plans Losing Appeal*, Korea Economic Daily, September 25, 2024

What We Eat

John Hooper, *THE ITALIANS*, MATI Publishing, 2017
Jeong Mi-ha, *Korea Ranks as the World's No. 1 Importer of U.S. Beef for Three Consecutive Years*, ChosunBiz, February 20, 2024
Korea Heritage Agency, *A Taste of Spring: Korean Wild Greens*, April 7, 2018
https://kh.or.kr/brd/board/741/L/menu/740?brdType=R&thisPage=1&bbIdx=105676&searchField=&searchText=

I Am From

Han Young-woo, *A Review of History*, Kyeongsewon, 1997
Neil MacGregor, *Germany: Memories of a Nation*, Penguin

Books, 2016

Four Kingdoms over Twenty Centuries

Benedict Anderson, *Imagined Communities: Reflections on the Origin and Spread of Nationalism*, Verso, 1983
Han Young-woo, *A Review of History*, Kyeongsewon, 1997

True Freedom Beyond Anti-communism

Park Jeong-ho, *They opposed everything*, YouTube, December 1, 2023
https://youtu.be/f_8VpADN1kE?si=QMtj4B5X0nYVEPCa
Han Young-woo, *A Review of Korean History*, Kyeongsewon, 1997

Rich out of Poverty

Soh, Hoon Sahib, Youngsun Koh, and Anwar Aridi (eds.). 2023. *Innovative Korea: Leveraging Innovation and Technology for Development.* Washington, DC: World Bank.
https://openknowledge.worldbank.org/handle/10986/40234

Believer Below 40%

Kim Hye-Young, *As Secularization Accelerates, How Are the Three Major Religious Groups Responding?*, Catholic Peace Broadcasting, November 11, 2024
Father Song Young-Oh, *AVE MARIA*, Gyeonggi Daily, June 10, 2014
https://www.kyeonggi.com/article/201406100579511

Beyond The Uniform

Kim Beom-Soo, *Perceptions of Unification (2024 Unification Awareness Survey)*, Seoul National University Institute for Unification and Peace Studies, October 2, 2024

Printed in Dunstable, United Kingdom